D0354400

A Little Book of Love

A Little Book
of Love

Heart Advice on
Bringing Happiness
to Ourselves and
Our World

MOH HARDIN

SHAMBHALA · *Boston & London* · 2011

Shambhala Publications, Inc.
Horticultural Hall
300 Massachusetts Avenue
Boston, Massachusetts 02115
www.shambhala.com

9   8   7   6   5   4   3   2   1

First Edition
Printed in the United States of America

✪This edition is printed on acid-free paper that meets the
American National Standards Institute Z39.48 Standard.
♻This book is printed on 30% postconsumer recycled paper.
For more information please visit www.shambhala.com.

Distributed in the United States by Random House, Inc.,
and in Canada by Random House of Canada Ltd

Designed by James D. Skatges

Library of Congress Cataloging-in-Publication Data
Hardin, Moh.
A little book of love: heart advice on bringing happiness
to ourselves and our world / Moh Hardin.—1st ed.
   p.   cm.
Includes bibliographical references.
ISBN 978-1-59030-900-1 (hardcover: alk. paper)
1. Love—Religious aspects—Buddhism. I. Title.
BQ4570.L6H37 2011
294.3′5677—dc22
2011012952

This book is dedicated to everyone
who has helped me learn about love.

I would especially acknowledge and thank my teachers,
Chögyam Trungpa and Sakyong Mipham,
my parents, Wannamaker and Margaret Hardin,
my former wives, Carol Jean and Judith,
my children, Justin and Cecily, and my step-son, Evan,
my cats, El Salvador and Boo,
and all beings.

Each of you has been my teacher.

This book is also very much a love song for my wife,
Sangyum Cynde Grieve.

It is in this way that we must train ourselves: by liberation of the self through love. We will develop love, we will practice it, we will make it both a way and a basis, take our stand upon it, store it up, and thoroughly set it going.

—THE BUDDHA

Contents

Introduction: The Way of Love   1

PART 1: STARTING AT HOME

1. Being Your Own Best Friend   9
2. Loving Your Partner   29
3. Loving Your Child   43

PART 2: THINKING BIGGER

4. The Power of a Wish   57
5. True Bravery   87
6. Love and Loyalty   107

Acknowledgments   131
Notes   133
Resources   137
About the Author   143

A Little Book of Love

Introduction

The Way of Love

THIS IS A LITTLE BOOK about a big word: *love*. Love plays an essential role in all of the world's great religions. It is also mentioned in the titles of pornographic sites on the Internet. It can refer to the unconditional love of parents for their children and to someone's love of peach ice cream. We talk about falling in love and falling out of love, as if it were a bed. Being in love can cause tremendous happiness and incredible pain. People can be blinded by love, or they can possess vast vision because of love. People can be ruthless because they are in love with power, and people can perform extraordinary acts of kindness out of love. *Love* is a big word that can be used to refer to many different experiences.

Love is also a big word in the sense that what love really is, the true nature of love, is beyond our ideas about it, beyond the ability of the human mind to conceive. Love cannot be grasped or possessed. Love is not a thing that can be measured. Love is like an ember in the heart of all human beings that, although it can be covered over, cannot be extinguished.

Every human being experiences love. This book contains practical advice from the Buddhist tradition about how to cultivate that love, how to deepen it, bring it out, and let it flower in our lives. In the Buddhist tradition, love is an immense concept—larger, perhaps, than our everyday thinking about it. Love is not just a feeling we have toward our spouse, our family, or our friends. It includes these relationships, of course, but love is a way of being present and awake in the world altogether.

A LITTLE BACKGROUND

I've been studying, practicing, and teaching Buddhism for roughly forty years. Like many American Buddhists, I didn't start out in this spiritual tradition.

I was born the son of a Methodist minister in South Carolina. As a young man, I met a remarkable Tibetan Buddhist teacher named Chögyam Trungpa. I studied with him for many years, and then with his son, Sakyong Mipham.

These teachers welcomed me into a venerable tradition of love and wisdom that began twenty-five hundred years ago when the Buddha attained enlightenment. *Buddha* is a Sanskrit word that literally means "the one who woke up." What did he wake up from? He woke up from confusion and pain, and transformed it into wisdom. Then, because people had questions, the Buddha began to teach.

The Buddha did not teach a belief system or a philosophy. He taught others how to discover, or uncover, and personally experience the awakened state of mind. How did he do that? All of his teachings can be divided into two categories: skillful means and wisdom. In teaching skillful means, the Buddha gives us things we can do, specific practices. These are like tools we can use for accomplishing a job. By using the tools described in this book, we awaken our own intelligence and confidence. We unlock our inherent love and our wisdom. This book is full of things you can do, and it describes the wisdom that will arise when you do them. The rest is up to you.

ABOUT THIS BOOK

This book is for anyone who is open to exploring a few basic tools and wisdoms from the Buddhist tradition for awakening, deepening, and expanding love in our lives and in our world. You don't have to be a Buddhist to read this book or apply these insights.

This book also tells the story of a journey—the journey of a bodhisattva, or an awake being. This journey begins with who we are this very moment. From this starting point, love is a journey outward. The destination is awakening to the magic of each moment and the inherent wisdom we possess. A bodhisattva makes this journey to benefit all beings who make this earth their home.

The basic logic of this journey is that to cultivate love and think bigger, it is important to start at home, making friends with ourself and opening to those around us. We can then expand our experience of love step-by-step. At the same time, we can cultivate more and more subtle tools with which to engage our world. This gives us the strength and wisdom to be fully awake and alive, which benefits both ourself and others.

Love has tremendous power to transform—people, families, communities, and nations. There is always room for more love and understanding in our world, from personal relationships to world politics. These relationships are all interconnected, so a little drop of love, of opening and welcoming others—at breakfast or in the middle of the afternoon—changes the world.

I believe in the little-drop approach. The forces of aggression and greed have a lot of strength in the world these days. Every time we add a drop of love, of caring, of deeper understanding, we are countering those forces and establishing a world based on friendship and openness. Each little drop is so very important.

Throughout this book, you'll find short highlighted sections called "Bringing It into Our Experience." These sections describe something you can do to bring the principles that are being discussed into your life. If what is said in a chapter or a section makes sense to you, then try the exercise or practice in "Bringing It into Our Experience." If you find this tool, this skillful means, beneficial and trustworthy, you might want to make it part of your life in an ongoing way.

I hope you enjoy *A Little Book of Love*. The teachings that I offer here are the Buddhist teachings that penetrated my own heart and mind, that helped me and provided fuel for my ongoing journey. One of the inspirations for writing this book was the thought that I'm growing older, and in this life I've had the opportunity to study with two realized teachers. What would I like to leave behind me as a testament and a token of gratitude? In response, I wrote this book. It is my aspiration that sharing these teachings will in some small way repay the kindness of my teachers and that the circle of love and wisdom will continue to expand.

PART ONE

Starting at Home

Being Your Own Best Friend

ACCORDING TO THE Buddhist tradition, if we want to cultivate love and deepen relationships or if we want to attain enlightenment, in both cases it is important that we begin by being friends with ourself. These days many people are quite hard on themselves. Whether or not you feel successful, you can still be quite hard on yourself. I speak with many people who appear—from the outside, at least—to have everything they could want, but they are not satisfied, and they sense that something is missing. Many of us believe that there is something lacking in ourselves and in our lives, that something is not quite right. As a result, we give ourselves a hard time. We are not living up to the image we have of what our lives should be.

This kind of self-judgment is the opposite of making friends with ourself. It is interesting that many people find it easier to be friends with someone else than with themselves. When we have a friend, it is usually because we like the way that person is. We get along with them and enjoy spending time with them. Then, maybe, they do something we don't like, and so we reject them—they are no longer our friend. We avoid them; we never want to see them again. That kind of friendship is based on certain conditions—our friend being a certain way—and when these conditions are not met, we reject the friendship.

If friendship with ourself is based on conditions, such as living up to a certain image of ourself, and then we do or think something we don't like, something we're not proud of, we might want to reject that part of ourselves, avoid it, and never see "that person" again. But the thing is, we are stuck with ourselves. We can try to run away, but wherever we go, we'll be there. Every morning when we look in the mirror, there we are again. So if we really want to make friends with ourself, that friendship has to be *un*conditional.

Unconditional friendship means that your friendship with yourself is not based on any conditions or on a certain image. It means that you can be friends with yourself even when you don't like yourself. That's outrageous, you say; it's a contradiction. How can you be friends with yourself when you don't like yourself?

Actually, that's the only place you can start. If you are going to wait to be friends with yourself until you live up to the image of who you think you should be, get rid of all the dark corners and are perfect, it will never happen. We are not talking about making friends with yourself as you would like to be, but as you are.

We could take, for example, a mother who has unconditional love for her child. She walks into a room where the child has been playing and has made a big mess. The mother thinks, "Oh!" in astonishment, and then, because she loves her child, her attitude quickly changes to "I see what's happened here." That "I see" is the key—it acknowledges that the child has made a mess, but also that the mother understands. The mother might experience irritation, but she has unconditional love for who the child is.

When we speak of unconditional friendship with ourself, we are looking at ourself and thinking, "Oh. I see." That "I see" is honest. We might not like everything we see, but behind that "I see" there is an unconditional acceptance of and friendship with who we are.

You might ask, "Is unconditional friendship with myself really such a good idea? If I make friends with myself as I am, accept myself as I am, there will be no reason to change or to improve myself, and I can just continue doing all the bad things I do."

In response I would ask, is that really friendship? If you have a friend who is doing something that causes harm to himself or is hurting others, wouldn't you try to help him stop doing that, help him to change? You would do this for the very reason that you are his friend. Likewise, if you can be friends with yourself as you are, of course you would still like to see yourself be the best you can be.

Perhaps you are in a bad situation or an unhealthy relationship. Making friends with yourself does not mean that you should not take steps to change the situation—either to improve it or to leave it. When we talk about unconditional friendship, we are not talking about not changing, we are talking about the starting point, the basic motivation for making a change. If you are making a change because you are your own best friend, then you will accomplish something meaningful. If you are trying to change yourself because you don't like yourself, you are picking up the wrong end of the stick, so to speak, and you will just keep beating yourself up with it.

DEVELOPING A DIFFERENT VIEW

Whether we think about it or not, we all have a *view:* an understanding of who we are, why we're here, and how the world works. We might believe that we are created by God or that we just randomly occurred. We might believe that we are a result of all our previous actions and intentions (what Buddhists call *karma*). There are many different ways we can see ourself, and this is what is meant by a view. Making friends with ourself has very much to do with how we see ourself and the world. For example, and to provide some reference points, I would like to briefly describe three views of reality, any and all of which might have influenced how we see ourself.

The first is the widely held view of original sin. According to *Merriam-Webster's Collegiate Dictionary,* eleventh edition, *original sin* is "the state of sin that according to Christian theology characterizes all human beings as a result of Adam's fall." According to this view, there is a basic inherited badness in us at birth that needs to be kept under control or fixed, rooted out. Guilt generally plays an important role in this view. How we handle this conflict between good and evil in this, our one lifetime on earth, will determine whether we spend eternity in heaven or hell.

Of course original sin is just one aspect of the Christian worldview. Christianity contains many wonderful teachings on love, and love plays a key role in Christian life. Here I am highlighting those views that might affect how we think and feel about ourselves.

The second widely held view is that of science and materialism. According to this view, we are simply the result of a random coming together of the DNA of an egg and a sperm. The purpose of life is to enjoy it while it lasts, perhaps produce children to carry our family into the future, amass material possessions, and accrue as much security as possible. When we die, we simply cease to exist. Since love cannot be substantiated or measured by scientific instruments, it does not play an important role in this view, other than perhaps as a mechanism for ensuring reproduction and the continuation of the species.

A third view is that of Buddhism. The teachings in this book are based on this view, so I will describe it in more detail. According to the Buddhist understanding, our basic nature is awake, or enlightened, and has been so forever. This is called our *buddha nature*, and all beings possess this awake quality. My teacher, Chögyam Trungpa, coined the term *basic goodness* to express in English this fundamental nature of our being. *Basic* means that this awakened nature that lies at our core is not dependent on any conditions, such as whether we are poor or rich, healthy or sick. It is more basic than that, or unconditional. It is original.

This basic nature never changes. Anything that relies on conditions is always changing. Take the weather, for example. The interactions of many different conditions—highs, lows, temperature, winds, and so forth—give us days of good weather and bad weather, and it is never the same for very long. If one condition, such as the temperature, changes by a degree, it affects everything else. Whether the days are sunny or stormy, however, up above the clouds, the sun itself doesn't change. It remains the sun unconditionally. It just is and does not change.

Like the sun, our basic nature never changes, and this never-changing nature is *goodness*. In the Buddhist view, the ultimate nature of reality is all good; this is a goodness that goes beyond our everyday concepts of good and bad.

Basic goodness is the natural, clear, and uncluttered state of our being that is always at our core. It is natural in the sense that it does not have to be created or maintained in any way. It is already here. It is clear because it perceives perfectly, without any distortions, whatever is happening at this very moment, like a flawless digital video camera. It is uncluttered because it is empty of all the schemes and paranoia of the ego's story lines.

This basic goodness naturally possesses qualities such as love, compassion, intelligence, gentleness, and wisdom. It is inseparable from these qualities, just as the sun is inseparable from its light and its warmth. In the Buddhist view, confusion and suffering arise from separating ourselves from the basic goodness of all life and becoming attached to protecting the sense of a separate self. Buddhists call this process *ego*. Another way we can describe ego is to say that we tend to build a kind of fortress around ourself that we think will protect us from life's upsets and sorrows, but in fact it inhibits our ability to love and causes us to suffer more.

Feeling the need to protect ourself gives rise to negative emotions such as anger and jealousy, but these emotions are not our true nature. Although they can grip us strongly, in reality, negative emotions are not who we are. They are like passing clouds in the sky. These clouds can cover the sun, but they never affect the sun. As soon as there is a gap in the clouds, the light and warmth of the sun shine through.

How do we uncover and bring out this basic goodness? That is what this little book is about. That is what all of the teachings of the Buddha are about. The way we begin is by cultivating unconditional friendship with ourself. We are worthy people. We deserve our own friendship. Although we may have learned to be hard on ourselves, it does not have to be this way. In our original nature it is not this way. Our true nature is good, just as the sun is naturally warm and bright. Cultivating that attitude, we can learn to be our own best friend.

A GESTURE OF FRIENDSHIP

It's like this. If we've had a bad day and are feeling flustered, angry, and upset, and while we are in that state of mind a mother asks us to hold her newborn baby, we would naturally hold the infant gently. Why? Because that newborn life is so obviously precious and fragile. Likewise, no matter how difficult our problems seem, no matter what obstacles we face, our lives are actually precious and fragile, just like that baby. Our lives are precious because we experience love, and we learn and grow. Our lives are fragile because we are all going to die, and the time of our death is unknown.

We have grown up and are no longer babies, but these fundamental qualities of our lives—precious and fragile—have not changed. So rather than be hard on ourselves, we can still hold ourselves with gentleness. We can respond to our own feelings and experiences as if we were picking up a newborn baby. We can be that gentle with ourself.

Cultivating an attitude that we are worthy of our own friendship is helpful, but sometimes we need something that we can actually do, a tool or a technique that helps us to accomplish our task. To become your own best friend, a useful tool is *making a gesture of friendship to yourself.* A gesture of friendship, like any gesture, is not just going to happen on its own—you have to make the gesture. What we're talking about here, though, is an internal gesture: you can't see it, but you can feel it.

It's helpful to compare this internal gesture of friendship to an external, physical gesture—such as the way you would gesture for someone to enter a doorway before you. A simple gesture of the hand and arm conveys "You are there. Please go first. I will follow." When you do this, you assume a certain posture; perhaps you turn your head and your body toward the other person with a slight bow for "You are there." Then there is the gesture itself, the movement of the hand and arm for "Please go first." Then the gesture ends in a different posture for "I will follow." Making a gesture of friendship to ourselves has the same sort of steps.

Step 1: Acknowledge What You Feel in This Moment

In making an internal gesture of friendship, we begin by acknowledging our own presence and getting our attention. This means that the first step is to feel ourself, however we might feel.

Be aware of yourself from the top of your head down though your body to your feet and your contact with the earth. Very quickly, like the brush of a feather, scan your body and be aware of how you feel: good, bad, emotional, depressed, angry, in love, anxious, peaceful—whatever it might be. Allowing yourself to feel yourself is in itself gentleness. Nothing extra called *gentleness* has to be added. That is the initial posture: "I am here, and I feel like this."

There is often a misconception that gentleness is an expression of weakness, but this gentle posture of acknowledging how you feel is one of strength. Why? Because you are brave enough not to hide from yourself. We can go to great lengths to avoid how we actually feel: keeping busy, losing ourselves in entertainments, blaming others for our troubles, daydreaming about how it could be—all kinds of things. To actually feel how you feel is a brave thing to do. "I am here. I feel the way I do." From this posture of bravery, gentleness, and strength, you can be kind to yourself.

Step 2: Extend Kindness to Yourself

In the external doorway gesture, from the initial posture of acknowledging the other person, you move your hand and arm in a sweeping gesture of opening, inviting the other person to go through the doorway before you. "You are there. Please go first." Likewise, from the posture of "I am here. I feel the way I do," you can make a gesture of kindness to yourself. Kindness feels soft, not hard. Kindness is, if just for a moment, free of heavy-handed judgment, and it includes acceptance, intelligence, and love.

It might sound strange to talk about loving yourself. But the word *love* can have different meanings, as we discussed earlier. We are not talking about loving ourselves in the sense of being vain, arrogant, or self-centered. We are talking about making a gesture of kindness, which is an expression of unconditional love.

We might not say, "I love my friend." Love is too strong a word, too potent. We would be more likely to say, "I like my friend" or "I care about my friend." But if we think of love beyond the romantic idea, we can safely say that love lies at the heart of every friendship. It is not a possessive love, but a more open love. When we are with a friend, we can relax and be ourselves. *Friendship* is an excellent word to express the experience of cultivating loving-kindness toward ourself—unconditional friendship that expresses itself as kindness.

A student of mine once described extending kindness to herself like this: "I think of a friend who is having a difficult time and of how I respond to her. Then I look at how hard I'm being on myself and realize I could never treat my friend the way I'm treating myself. I would never be so hard on her. I would see her suffering, I might pat her on the back or hug her, and I would say something kind."

Step 3: Experience the Warmth of Friendship

When someone is kind to us, it generates an experience of warmth. It might be a very simple thing: a word of kindness, helping us to complete a task, or simply being there for us without judgment. Or simpler still, let's look at our doorway example from another point of view: If someone pushes ahead of us to go through the door first, it makes us feel bad. It may hurt our feelings a little bit or make us angry. If instead the person gestures us to go first, that little acknowledgement can produce a feeling of warmth and friendship, even if we don't know the person. Perhaps we stand up a little straighter. We feel good, even if just for an instant. Likewise, the result of making a gesture of kindness to ourselves is the warmth of friendship.

This experience of warmth might be an almost physical sensation. For some people, it might be very subtle. "Feeling alive" might be another way to describe it. Sometimes you might not feel anything in particular, but you are simply more present than you were before you made this gesture toward yourself. A friend recently told me that he kept expecting a feeling like you might have for your mother or your lover, but then he realized that the result of making gestures of friendship toward himself was different from that. Instead, he found that the decisions he was making about his life day by day were changing and becoming more and more an expression of being his own best friend.

Whatever the experience is, it is important to acknowledge it and let it go. You can't hold on to it, anymore than you would want to freeze in time and space at the end of gesturing someone through the door. The gesture has been made. It's just a little moment in your life. The point is to keep walking.

The habit of being hard on ourselves can be deeply engrained, so one gesture will not undo years and years of training. This is why in the Buddhist tradition we talk about a path or a journey of restoring our well-being. The ground on which this journey takes place is being our own best friend. We therefore need to repeat the gesture of friendship again and again, intentionally cultivating the habit of being kind to ourselves.

Bringing It into Our Experience
A Gesture of Friendship

If we want to deepen and expand our loving, making an internal gesture of friendship to ourself is a useful tool. This tool works in three stages:

1. Acknowledge yourself and how you feel.
2. Be kind to whatever you find.
3. Experience the resulting warmth of friendship.

Once you become familiar with this gesture of friendship, it will be a quick, simple gesture that you can make to yourself many times a day.

SPENDING TIME WITH YOURSELF

If you are interested in someone and want to make friends with him or her, the first thing you try to do is spend time with that person. Likewise, if you want to make friends with yourself, the most powerful way for

23

that to occur is, quite simply, to spend time with your-self. The age-old practice of sitting meditation is a great way of spending quality time with yourself.

Simply sit down with yourself in a comfortable, up-right, and attentive posture, as if you are on a date with someone whom you are very curious to get to know. Sit with yourself with that kind of attention.

Of course we are with ourselves all the time in some way, but usually we are busy doing something, we are distracted, or we want to be entertained. We know what we like and don't like, but do we really know ourself? Are we friends with ourself?

Take just a few minutes each day to be with your-self in a simple way, without busyness, distractions, or entertainment. Just sit down and be. How does this work? First, it's important to take a good seat. This means being purposeful and deliberate about where and how we sit. Sit in a quiet place where you won't be distracted. You can sit on a chair or a meditation cushion. Assume an erect, comfortable posture. Dur-ing sitting practice, our upright posture will provide a reminder of what we're doing, of our noble commit-ment to simply be for a while.

Having taken your seat, keep your eyes open with-out necessarily looking around. Become aware of the environment: the space around you, the room you are sitting in. Then direct your focus to your breathing. The breath is a manifestation of being alive, and it always takes place in the present moment. When we place our attention on the breath, we synchronize our mind with the present moment. We become aware of being alive.

Resting on the breath, on the present moment, is like sitting on an island in the midst of a rushing river. Up to now we have been swept along with the current, not having any idea how fast we were going. Now we have a reference point, a still point, and it's as if we are sitting on an island in the river. We can watch the currents of thoughts and emotions flow past. Generally, there are quite a lot of them. We will be swept away by them again and again, but by coming back to the breath, the island of the present moment, we will begin to gain a bigger and clearer perspective on the currents of our life.

By providing time in our lives for simply sitting, we become more aware, not less. Sometimes the open time of meditation allows an uncomfortable memory or feeling to surface. This is similar to the process of making friends with someone else. Perhaps at first our new friend tells us only the good stuff, but as we spend more time with her or him and become closer friends, if we really get to know this person, there is always something painful that eventually emerges. The same will be true of ourselves: we will see the good and the bad. The mind of friendship can encompass all of it.

I would like to say that taking some time each day with yourself in this way is the kindest thing you could ever do for yourself. It will also benefit your family, your friends, and everyone you love.

Bringing It into Our Experience
Ten-Minute Sitting Meditation

In a quiet, undistracted place,

1. Take your seat.
2. Be aware of the room and the space around you.
3. Make a gesture of friendship to yourself.
4. Place your awareness on the flow of your breathing. Identifying with the present moment in this way; watch the currents of thoughts, emotions, and worries rush by.

Many times you will be swept away in the currents, but the breath is always there, so you can come back to it again and again—it is a resting place.

After ten minutes, look around the room and slowly get up.

Try to do this daily. Ten minutes is suggested,

but it may be shorter or longer, depending on your circumstances.

THE JOURNEY OF FRIENDSHIP

Making friends with ourself is not a one-shot deal—you do it and it's done. Nor is it a project that is going to take a week or even a year. You might experience some benefits almost immediately from sitting meditation and from making gestures of friendship to yourself. But these skillful means are not particularly meant as a quick fix, but as a way to proceed, a path. They each take place in the present moment, so they are always up-to-date. It is in the present that the journey of friendship unfolds. This journey of friendship with ourself is not based on trying to change ourselves because we are bad and should be good. It is not based on trying to change ourselves because we don't have something and need to get it, nor is it based on getting rid of something we shouldn't have. This journey of friendship is traditionally referred to as a *journey of transformation*, and transformation is different from changing because we want to become better. Transformation is a natural process that arises from basic goodness; it is a process of uncovering what we most truly are and letting it shine.

In this chapter we have discussed two helpful tools to use on the continuing journey of being our own best friend: making a gesture of friendship to ourselves in any given moment, and synchronizing our body and mind in the present moment in sitting meditation. The principles we learn from using these tools—being kind to ourselves and simply being present—will be helpful on whatever journey we take. It may be a business venture, a love affair, a spiritual quest, or just getting up in the morning to start a new day. I can personally say that whenever I have remembered the two principles of being kind and present, they have always been relevant and helpful.

Loving Your Partner

I F YOU LOVE YOUR PARTNER—your husband, wife, or lover—from my experience I would say that the most important ingredient for a good, healthy, and long-lasting relationship is space. We can learn how to give each other the gift of space.

What do I mean by "giving space"? We often respond to situations with a kind of knee-jerk reaction. This is because there is no space in which to see that we have alternatives, no space in which awareness can take place. We are caught in our habitual reactions and patterns. For example, perhaps we like to fold the laundry a certain way. We do it this way because it is obviously superior. If our partner folds it differently, we immediately get irritated and tell them how they should do it. At that moment, we are not really relating to our partner, but to our own irritation. We cannot see our partner at all. We are caught in a habitual response.

Giving space can simply mean pausing a little before we burst out, creating a little gap in which we can notice our partner or friend in that present moment. This has nothing to do with "spacing out." It's much clearer and more purposeful than that. Rather than immediately reacting the same way we always have, space creates the potential for something new to happen. It is an openness out of which possibilities occur.

One way to think about space is that it gives perspective. If we are wandering in a deep, thick forest, there is not enough space around us to see where we are, and it is easy to get lost. If we climb up to an open meadow at the top of a mountain and look out over the hills and valleys, we gain a bigger perspective. From that big view, we can best choose the way to go.

The practice of sitting meditation described in chapter 1 is a way to cultivate space or perspective in our lives. Coming back again and again to the present moment, making friends with ourself, having that reference point, gives us a different perspective from the one we have when we are simply swept along by life's currents. From our new vantage point, we can see how the currents interconnect and interrelate. We begin to get a picture of the whole river.

In relationships, space reduces friction and creates the room for us to dance together. Of course, space isn't the only ingredient in a healthy, lasting relationship. If space were the only ingredient, nothing would ever happen. But in a relationship where there is space, the dynamic energies of love, attachment, and emotions can balance themselves more naturally, and the relationship has a more stable basis from which to endure the ups and downs, the ins and outs of love.

When we fall in love, and especially when we make a long-term or lifelong commitment to a relationship, the other person becomes one of the most significant influences in our lives. Our lives are enmeshed and entangled. In that context, what does it mean to give one's partner the gift of space?

Meditation master Chögyam Trungpa said, "Being in love does not mean possessing the other person; it simply means appreciating the other person." The difference between love based on trying to possess someone and love based on appreciating someone is immense, if you think about it. Trying to possess the ones we love takes away their freedom. We imprison them in our idea of who we think they are, who we want or need them to be. This prison provides little room for their self-expression and growth, because we have already filled up all the space.

Appreciating our partners, on the other hand, is to see them as they are, to be open to them as they are. It may be as simple as appreciating the way they do something around the house, rather than criticizing them for not doing it the way we would. This provides them the space for growth, the space for them to express themselves. So appreciating your partner rather than possessing him or her is one way to give the gift of space.

A FLASH OF GENEROSITY

Another way to give the gift of space is to "flash" generosity to your partner. When you see your partner or your friend, just take a moment, inwardly, to open to him or her, to who that person is in that moment. Open beyond your preconceived ideas, as if you've never seen this person before. It's a moment of being fresh and receptive to your partner. You're giving the gift of space. Then just carry on with whatever you were doing. This flash of generosity is just a little gap in the flow of your day. Don't try to make it into something momentous, and don't try to hold on to it. Just flash generosity and let it go.

This flash of generosity starts within and is a journey outward. It's very quick, like the lightbulb flash of a camera in a darkened room. It's a sudden glimpse of your partner as they are in that moment.

Here's how it happens, in slow motion:

1. Contact a sense of friendship and warmth within yourself.
2. Expand this warmth outward, melting your fixed ideas and creating a little gap in which you can experience the uncluttered openness of basic goodness.
3. The result is natural, clear awareness—the open space for genuine communication.

With this precise instruction, we can explore this journey step-by-step—friendship within, expanding outward, and opening to the world around us—and see how it works. We can play with it in our experience. As we become more familiar with it in slow motion, it's easier to just flash generosity.

Of course, this flash can be toward anyone at any time, but here we are talking about it specifically as a way of giving the gift of space to your partner or your friend.

Bringing It into Our Experience
Starting Today, Flash Generosity

When you see your partner or your friend, just for a flash, see him or her in a fresh way. Contact warmth, expand it outward, and rest in awareness. Do this as often as you can remember.

BODHICHITTA

This flash of generosity, of opening beyond your fixed ideas and welcoming your partner or your friend as he or she is, is an example of *bodhichitta*. *Bodhichitta* is a Sanskrit word. *Bodhi* means "awake," and *chitta* can be translated as "mind" or "heart." So *bodhichitta* means "awakened mind" and "awakened heart." Normally we associate the word *mind* with the intellect and the word *heart* with feelings and intuition. If I say that you have an open mind, it has certain connotations. If I say that you have an open heart, it means something different. *Bodhichitta* is an open mind *and* an open heart together, inseparable—one experience. Rather than living in your own dream world, your mind and your heart are open and awake.

Flashing generosity provides a sudden glimpse of your partner that is fresh because it is uncluttered by your projections onto them, which in turn frees us from being stuck in our habitual reactions to them. It opens up space, and it is the first step in a journey outward. It is most appropriate that this first step, this flash of generosity, be toward someone we love. We can often learn the most from the people we love the most, because we can dare to open to them beyond our habitual patterns and expectations.

Giving the gift of space creates doorways for open, spontaneous communication. Of course you know this person, you know him or her well, and of course you are going to have your idea of who they are. You are also going to want them to behave in certain ways. These expectations and projections will continue. We are not talking about getting rid of anything. We are talking about flashing generosity in the midst of whatever is already happening.

This creates magic, the magic of bodhichitta, of the awakened heart and mind. Each flash of generosity opens a little gap in the flow of habitual responses and creates freshness and potential. Bodhichitta does not change everything all at once; it is the drop-by-drop approach. Rather than coasting along in old patterns, flashing generosity creates gaps in which up-to-date communication can occur. Without your trying to change anything, things change of their own accord.

Good communication lies at the heart of a healthy relationship, and like learning to dance, communication requires space and time. We are not talking about trying to force communication on our partners or forcing something out of them. We can't make others communicate with us the way we want them to. That is not communication but manipulation. When we flash generosity, in little drops, we are letting go of manipulation. In little drops, we are daring to be open. In little drops, we are learning to love more deeply.

LISTENING AND SPEAKING

We communicate with those we love in many ways, but language—how we speak and listen—is fundamental in understanding each other. In order to fully cultivate the openness of bodhichitta in our relationships, let's talk a little about talking.

Right speech was taught by the Buddha as a way to bring peace to oneself and one's world. Right speech is saying what is true. Speaking that which is true doesn't mislead or confuse others. It is genuine and trustworthy, and so it cultivates peace.

Right speech includes refraining from saying what is not true. Lying or misleading in order to benefit ourselves—and that is almost always our motivation for lying—destroys any chance for open, genuine communication. We are creating a reality that is untrue, out of tune with basic goodness, and this makes it impossible to find real peace. When we have something to hide, we cannot be open.

Saying what is true prepares the ground of trust on which good, open communication can take place. On that ground of right speech, in order for our own speech to be effective, it is also important to cultivate skill in listening. Listening is actually the key to effective speech.

Often, when we appear to be listening, we are really thinking about what we are going to say next. That is not really listening; it is talking to ourselves. It is like rehearsing, so that as soon as there is some space, we can fill it with our opinions or stories.

To truly listen is a skill we can develop, so it makes sense to work at it. This means putting our focused attention on what our partner or friend is saying, rather than listening to our thoughts about what we think about what they are saying. When we listen to our thoughts, we are several times removed from what's actually being said.

Perhaps it's obvious, but good communication relies on actually hearing what the other person is saying. We don't need to analyze it, nor do we need to frame responses. We can tell the commentator in our head to be quiet for a while. We can listen with our hearts to the feelings that are being expressed, as well as with our minds to the meaning. We don't need to fix or change anything about what the other person is feeling or thinking. We can stop and just listen to what our friend is saying.

By just listening, we can be spontaneous and genuine when we speak, responding appropriately, saying what we mean and meaning what we say. If we truly listen, and if we say what is true, our speech will be genuine. There is no trick, no one-upmanship, no deception. There is no book that can tell you what to say. Genuine speech has power because it is in tune with what is true in that very moment. It is a matter of trusting ourselves, trusting that what we say in the open space of bodhichitta will be the right thing, which means learning to trust our basic goodness.

We can also educate ourselves and increase our awareness by listening to ourselves when we are speaking. Ask yourself, "What is the tone of my voice? Are my words expressing what I am trying to say?" The purpose of doing this is not to become self-conscious but to cultivate mindfulness in our speech and awareness of the effect of our speech on others. That is how we learn and cultivate skill and wisdom.

Good communication will serve any relationship well. It can be delightful and playful, deep and sincere, or quite ordinary, depending on the circumstances. Genuine communication is always appropriate, always in tune.

TRUST

When there is space and good communication, what happens? You never really know—this is the spontaneity, the freshness of relationship. In the beginning, relationships are always fresh. There is an inherent sense of spontaneity as we discover each other. There is the excitement and joy of falling in love or making a new friend.

Any relationship is going to develop patterns and routines over time. The comfort and security we feel in a relationship is very much based on the patterns of how we relate to each other and how things get done. If the patterns work and satisfy the needs of both individuals, these habits become the bedrock on which the relationship can flourish.

Having patterns does not mean that there can't be spontaneity. You can flash generosity to your partner in the midst of doing the routine household chores, many times a day. This is not a duty; it's a delight. It brings the spontaneity of the present moment into play.

"But what if it's not a delight?" someone might ask. "What if I don't like what I see when I open to my partner?" There is always an aspect of clear seeing to bodhichitta. Flashing generosity, seeing through our own habits and expectations, also informs our opinions. Since we are going to have opinions anyway, they might as well be as close to reality as possible.

Seeing who is there, and not just our idea of who is there, is the wakeful quality of bodhichitta. In a good relationship, that kind of seeing brings appreciation. In an unhealthy relationship, it can help us to realize when a relationship is problematic.

To really fall in love with someone, you have to let down your guard. You will be vulnerable, not in the sense of weakness, but in the sense of being brave enough to be defenseless—to relax and let go. This requires trust. You must trust yourself, to begin with, and then it's a matter of opening outward and learning to trust your partner, your friend.

Trust is built over time. Trust is also quickly destroyed, and once destroyed can take a very long time to be restored. The best way to prevent this from happening is to not do anything untrustworthy. It is worthwhile to build a trusting relationship. It will enrich your life.

In this chapter, we have talked about the importance of space to support wakefulness in a living, changing relationship. We have described some tools for giving the gift of space in a relationship, including:

1. Cultivating appreciation of your partner for who they are, not who you think they should be
2. Flashing generosity
3. Skillfully listening and speaking

Of these three, the key instruction is the cultivation of bodhichitta by flashing generosity. This is supported by appreciating your partner, and it manifests in good communication.

We now have these three new tools at our disposal. Whenever we are given a new tool, we have to learn how to use it by trying it out and looking at the results. Initially we have to give a lot of care and attention to how we use it. Over time, as we become familiar with it, using the tool becomes natural.

I encourage you to start using these tools in your daily life, in your relationships. At first it might feel awkward. You might feel unsure of yourself. But with practice you will get better and better at warmly opening up a space for your partner to be who he or she is, and within that open space the dynamic dance of love will flourish.

Loving Your Child

THIS CHAPTER IS about children. It is written as though you are a parent, but it applies equally if you are a grandparent, an aunt or an uncle, a friend, a teacher, or a mentor. Children live in a special world of growth and discovery. The first two decades of our lives, more or less, are a time of constant growth, of both the body and the person—a period of discovery of who we are and how the world works and doesn't work.

From a Buddhist understanding, a newborn baby is not a blank slate. Babies bring certain qualities into the world with them. Two children born of the same parents and brought up in the same environment can be quite different. They each have their own karma. That is, they come into this world with certain propensities, certain styles of expression and intelligence, certain talents and interests. These propensities can make a child behave in ways we call good or bad, in the conventional sense, but the original nature of the child is always basic goodness.

Some situations nurture children's basic goodness and encourage their inherent curiosity, and some obscure it. Some incite hatred, and others nurture love. Some seek to mold the child in a certain way, and others give space for self-expression. Some nourish, and others ignore. There are many mixtures and gradations. The environment a child grows up in interacts with the child's propensities, and the two together create the person the child is and will be.

We love our children and want to do the best we can for them, so the question is how to apply our love for our children in our everyday life. In our relationship with our children, how do we communicate with their basic goodness and cultivate their confidence in their own worthiness? The raising of children is a vast topic, so I want to focus on this one essential question: How do we manifest our love for our children in day-to-day life?

In the previous chapter, we explored how to culti-vate a heart and mind that are open and awake through the practice of flashing generosity. This brings an experience of bodhichitta. Bodhichitta is an extraordinary, magical, and yet practical tool given to us by the Buddha to apply love in our lives and thoroughly get it going.

What is the relationship between bodhichitta and love? When you are in love, your heart and mind are naturally open and awake to life. When you cultivate bodhichitta by opening and awakening your heart and mind, love can flow and grow.

Bodhichitta is like opening the curtains, and love is like the sun shining through, bringing light and warmth into the room. Or we could say that bodhi-chitta is like opening the window, and love is the cool breeze that refreshes the stuffiness and stagnation of living inside a personal fortress. Bodhichitta is like discovering an inexhaustible treasure, and love is its enjoyment. Bodhichitta is our direct connection with basic goodness.

BASIC GOODNESS IN A GOOD AND BAD WORLD

The original nature of a child, a teenager, or, in fact, all people is basic goodness. Before the idea of good and bad arises, the nature of being is pure and spontaneously present. This basic goodness has never been stained by anything, in the same way that the sun, though obscured by clouds, has never been stained by the clouds.

We are so accustomed to defining *good* in relationship to *bad* that the notion of basic goodness is very difficult to grasp. When a child behaves badly, we might wonder, "Where is basic goodness?" Where is it when he is selfish, possessive, and refuses to share? Where is it when she tells a lie or refuses to listen? How can we communicate with children's basic goodness—touch it, draw it out, and let it shine through their preoccupation with their own little world?

As parents, we have to relate to the whole child, to the clouds and the sun, but it is so easy to see only the clouds and to get lost in ideas of good versus bad. Sometimes our children are good and sometimes they are bad, but if we can remember that their original nature is and has always been basic goodness, this will be most helpful to us. There is nothing that needs to be fixed, because nothing was ever broken. As parents, friends, teachers, and mentors, we must see past good versus bad. It is our task, our delightful duty, and our responsibility to touch a child's basic goodness.

The third Zen Buddhist patriarch, Master Sengstan (seventh-century China), is quoted as saying, "Do not seek perfection in a changing world. Instead perfect your love." There's a lot of wisdom in that quotation. It could apply to any love relationship, but it is especially relevant to how we relate to our children and other family members. This instruction from Master Sengstan points out how our families can teach us the most about love *by not being perfect.*

If we are seeking perfection in our children or in other family members, the chances are good that we are simply putting the people closest to us in our own movie. We, in the role of director, expect them to live up to our scripts and our agendas. Such heavy expectations do not cultivate an environment of open communication in which love, or a family, can grow and flourish.

Rather than measuring our children against our own expectations, we can open and see our sons and our daughters as they are, which opens the floodgates of love. Our children then become our guides in teaching us how to perfect our love rather than seeking to perfect them. They become our friends in helping us to cultivate bodhichitta, the awakened heart and mind. We can grow as our children grow. We are on a journey together. In fact, growing is what healthy families do—not just the children, but the parents, too.

COMMUNICATING WITH A CHILD'S BASIC GOODNESS

As we have discussed, cultivating bodhichitta by flashing generosity provides a glimpse of another person that is natural, clear, and uncluttered by our expectations and projections. It happens very quickly, as just a glimpse of the clear, uncluttered space of basic goodness. This flash is a journey out of our fortress of preferences and opinions. Bodhichitta opens the space in which love can flow, grow, and flourish. Let's look again at this flash of generosity as it might be applied to our children:

1. Contact a sense of presence, friendship, and warmth within yourself.
2. Expand that friendship and warmth outward to your child, not just as a thought but like a wave that originates in your heart and melts your fixed ideas of what you are going to find.
3. The result can be a genuine encounter with your child.

The term *genuine encounter* comes from a book that my mother gave me when my first child was born: *Your Child's Self-Esteem* by Dorothy Corkille Briggs. I found a lot of helpful information in this book, but this idea of genuine encounter really jumped out at me and influenced me. It relates directly to the view of basic goodness and the practice of bodhichitta.

Briggs writes: "Every child needs periodic genuine encounters with his [or her] parents. Genuine encounter is simply focused attention . . . and being intimately open to the particular, unique qualities of your child."

She then gives an example of what she means by "focused attention":

Very young children demonstrate focused attention constantly. Watch a toddler as he spies a caterpillar. He becomes thoroughly absorbed in its fuzziness, its particular movements and way of eating. He is personally engaged with the 'particularness' of the caterpillar.

I can give a personal example of a genuine encounter. When my son Justin was a toddler, we lived in an old farmhouse in Vermont. Each morning we walked from the bedroom down a long narrow hallway that had wainscoting along the walls. I generally walked ahead, holding Justin's hand and gently pulling him along. He would always run his other hand along the grooves of the wainscoting. There was a hole in the wall at one place, and Justin always wanted to stop and explore it. I would pull him forward if we needed to get somewhere soon, because it seemed he could study this hole forever.

One morning, when I had been reading about genuine encounter and thinking about bodhichitta, I took a different approach. I tried running my hand along the wainscoting with him. At first I was very tentative, as though I wasn't sure what I was doing. But it was pretty cool, my fingers bouncing lightly along the grooves in rhythm. When we got to the hole, I stopped and watched Justin explore it. I gave him my focused attention. I saw his particular unique qualities in that moment. He positively glowed with curiosity.

This magical moment with my son influenced the way I related with my children from that time on. I encourage you to nurture genuine encounters with your child, to see him or her with fresh eyes, as he or she is in each moment. Flash generosity and appreciate your child's particular unique qualities. There is no one else like this child.

Bringing It into Our Experience
Flash Generosity to Your Child

Flash generosity to your children every time you see them. That way it will become a habit. It's not a big deal but a way of being, a spark of curiosity, an open doorway through which love can flow.

When you have young children, there is never a lack of opportunity to cultivate bodhichitta by flashing generosity and to create the openness in which a genuine encounter can take place. As children grow and become more independent, the practical challenge is to create an opportunity, a context, in which a genuine encounter can occur. Busy families can share a home yet actually spend very little time together.

It's important to find something to do with each of your children as they grow older, something that is regular and not a big deal but that gives you time together. Take your child out to lunch, walk the dog together, or something like that. It could be sharing a hobby, playing a sport together, or shopping—something you both enjoy. There are many options. The important thing is to keep pathways of communication open in which genuine encounters can occur.

A HEALTHY EGO

Genuine encounters with our children help them to develop healthy egos. You might ask, "If Buddhists view ego as the problem (*ego* defined as the sense of being separate from the basic goodness of all life), why are we talking about helping a child to develop a healthy ego?" The reason is that the experience a child has of being separate is very real, and this increases in the teenage years. It is therefore of the utmost importance that as parents we help to cultivate in our child a healthy sense of who he or she is as a unique individual.

How would I, as a Buddhist, define a healthy ego? A healthy ego has two qualities, both of which are expressions of the child's basic goodness: inwardly, there is a sense of worthiness; outwardly, there is an awareness of others.

When children feel acknowledged for who they are, when they feel respected, when discipline includes positive as well as negative feedback, when they have periodic genuine encounters with their parents, they feel loved and develop the sense that they are worthy of being alive and part of this world. Of course, every child will have positive experiences as well as negative experiences, times of success and fulfillment as well as times of disappointment and hurt. When children feel worthy deep inside, when they are connected with the basic nobility of the human spirit, basic goodness will give them strength and help carry them through the bad times and the good.

Is this not the deep wish of all parents? We can protect our children only so much in this world, but by communicating with their basic goodness, we can give them the gift and the strength of being worthy and unique human beings who can find their own way in the world.

On the outside, a child with a healthy ego acknowledges that other children or teenagers (and adults!) have real feelings, too, just as he or she does. Children can be so preoccupied with their own feelings that they never realize that other children have feelings, too, unless it's pointed out to them, sometimes repeatedly, with gentleness and love. If your child is selfish and will not share, if your teenager is angry and wants to hurt someone, the question you should pose is "How would you feel if someone did this to you?" Gentle persistence will gradually open children to a bigger world, to seeing beyond their own self-interest and feeling part of the basic goodness of all life.

Feeling worthy and seeing another's point of view are the elements of a healthy ego in a child or young adult. These two qualities will serve young people well throughout their lives. Parenting is not always easy, but it is my hope that the tools we have discussed here will give you a key to open the door through which your basic goodness can communicate with your child's basic goodness. I hope that you will make use of these tools so that you and your child can have periodic genuine encounters, surrounded by appreciation and communication. As you enjoy the great treasure of awakened heart and open mind, this will allow your love for your children to manifest in your day-to-day life. That is my wish for you.

Thinking Bigger

The Power of a Wish

LIFE IS A JOURNEY, whether we think about it that way or not. From moment to moment, new things happen to us, as if we were traveling down a path at once familiar and fresh, depending on how we see it and how we make use of it.

In part one, our discussions focused on two core teachings of the Buddha: the ongoing journey of unconditional friendship with ourself, and the bodhichitta practice of flashing generosity and opening to others. With bodhichitta, we especially focused on those closest to us because there is already a basis of love and intimacy. By cultivating gaps in our patterns and the space in which genuine encounter can occur, the tools of making a gesture of friendship to ourselves and flashing generosity to those we love will bring both immediate and long-term benefits.

The Buddha also understood that to bring the most lasting benefit to ourselves and others, there is a greater journey to be taken. This journey is based on thinking bigger—beyond our own personal happiness and the happiness of our families and friends. This greater journey involves wishing for the happiness of all beings. That is a big wish. It's an expression of love for all beings, excluding none, and this one simple wish has the power to transform our future.

PLANTING A GARDEN OF HAPPINESS

What we wish for is a powerful motivating force in our lives and ultimately shapes the world we live in. For example, you might wish to make a lot of money, and that aspiration motivates you to work hard, please your employer and your customers, and manage your investments well. It is not so much that you think every day, "I want to make a lot of money"; but that underlying aspiration gives rise to an enormous amount of focused activity in your day-to-day life and decisions.

Perhaps you wish to be helpful to others. You have chosen a career as a caregiver, a teacher, a health-care professional, or a counselor. Your aspiration to be helpful shapes what you do every day and the way you earn your living.

Or maybe you aspire to be an artist. You have something you wish to express, something you would like to share. Because of that, you spend hours every day practicing your discipline, be it painting, music, writing, or making movies. Again, you don't consciously think every day, "I want to be an artist." The wish to express your vision is simply always there, and your activity arises from that.

You are reading this book, so in you already is the desire to be happy and to bring happiness to others. The Buddha understood the deep aspiration people have for happiness, and he also understood that real happiness is the result of thinking bigger, beyond our ordinary ideas about where to find happiness. And so the Buddha gave us a set of tools called the Four Limitless Ones. These are love, compassion, joy, and equanimity, and they are sometimes called "the four that cannot be measured."

The Four Limitless Ones work at the ground level of what we wish for in our lives. What we wish for gives rise to our thoughts, and our thoughts motivate us to action. Our actions set other things in motion, in either positive or negative ways, which result in ourselves and others experiencing happiness or unhappiness. This is called *karma*: everything we do sets something else in motion. Since what we do arises from what we wish for, here we are talking about the very deep level in our being that gives rise to things, to activities. We are planting seeds there. By thinking deeply about equanimity, love, compassion, and joy, we are planting seeds in our minds and our hearts that will lead to happiness for ourselves and others.

If you want to grow a garden of good food, you would not plant seeds of crabgrass, stinging nettle, and other weeds. You would plant seeds of beans, cucumbers, tomatoes, and squash; these seeds would produce healthy plants, which in turn would bear delicious fruit. Likewise, if you want to plant a garden of happiness, you would not sow seeds of deception, anger, jealousy, and greed. If you plant seeds of equanimity, love, compassion, and joy, then these seeds will give rise to actions that benefit others, which in turn will bear the fruit of happiness for yourself, those you love, and all beings. That is the power of the Four Limitless Ones. That is the power of a wish.

THE BODHISATTVA PATH

The greater journey of thinking bigger is described in the teachings of the Buddha as the path of a bodhisattva. *Bodhisattva* is another Sanskrit word. *Bodhi* again means "awake," and *sattva* means "being," so *bodhisattva* simply means "awake being." A person who is awake does not live in a dream but is in touch with what is real. The key to the bodhisattva path, as well as what is cultivated on the path, is bodhichitta, the awakened mind and heart.

We have been introduced to bodhichitta in the practice of flashing generosity. Perhaps at this point bodhichitta is more than just a new word or an abstract idea; there may be some experience connected with it. Even if that experience is just a glimpse, an intuition, or an exploration, there is a relationship growing there, I hope. From that simple glimpse of opening outward, in whatever way you might understand or experience it, arises the bigger thinking of a bodhisattva.

As a potential bodhisattva, you begin to see through your own opinions and projections of who you think others are, and you see that beneath these projections there are real, living, changing human beings. Inspired by bodhichitta, which we could call "the mind of an awakened heart," a potential bodhisattva begins to think beyond his or her immediate preoccupations and happiness. They begin to understand more deeply the interconnection between *their* world and *the* world, and to have more confidence and trust in basic goodness. Inspired by many who have travelled on this path before, they give birth to the intent to open to reality and uncover wisdom for the benefit of all beings. This is how a bodhisattva is born.

The bodhisattva then sets out on a journey outward, a journey of discovery, of opening to him- or herself, to others, and to the larger world around us. The journey of a bodhisattva is powered by the intent to live fully with an open heart and mind for the benefit of all beings. The bodhisattva approaches the journey of life in such a way that it becomes a path of awakening and growth.

Why would anyone want to go on such a journey? There are many good reasons, which I hope will become clear as we describe this journey, but in essence there is a *spark*. That is the best way to say it: a spark of bodhichitta, a flash of opening. The great Buddhist poet Shantideva describes bodhichitta as being like "a flash of lightning on a dark night." For an instant, everything is illuminated. From that flash we are inspired to wake up and see further. This is the natural expression of basic goodness, of the sun shining through a gap in the clouds. It is the natural expression of love. Our curiosity is aroused, so we are naturally open to looking at things or thinking about things in a different way, perhaps, than we ever have before. We feel inspired to explore, to make our minds bigger, and to open our hearts.

Traditionally, the Four Limitless Ones are expressed with the following phrases or aspirations:

> *May all beings enjoy happiness and the root of happiness.*
> (Love)
> *May they be free from suffering and the root of suffering.*
> (Compassion)
> *May they not be separated from the great happiness devoid of suffering.* (Joy)
> *May they dwell in the great equanimity free from passion, aggression, and prejudice.* (Equanimity)

EQUANIMITY

Let's begin exploring the Four Limitless Ones with the one that comes last: equanimity. "Why start there?"

you might ask. If we want to generate love, compassion, and joy for all beings, if we're willing to go on this transformative journey, we're going to need to lay some groundwork within ourselves. We'll need a sense of balance, some evenness, and some peace—in other words, we'll need equanimity.

A good way to develop equanimity is by contemplating what we have in common with all other living beings. We tend to set ourselves apart, but here are six ways in which we are all equal.

Mothers

The traditional Buddhist teaching that is invoked to make our love bigger, to inspire love and compassion with impartiality toward all, is to see every being, be it an ant crawling on the ground or the president of a country, as having been our mother. Buddhists believe in rebirth; we have each lived innumerable lifetimes—not just as humans, but as all sorts of living things (snails, butterflies, mammals of all kinds, you name it). We've had so many different lives in so many different forms that at some point, every other being has been our mother—has given birth to us, nourished us, and loved us unconditionally. Therefore, we should regard all beings that we meet in our lives with the love and appreciation we feel toward our mother. Although someone may appear as an enemy in this lifetime, he or she was once our mother. All beings are equal in that way.

This is a beautiful image, based on quite a vast view of reality. Contemplating that all beings we meet have at some time been our mother is good because it stretches our minds. Nevertheless, this might not be an image that those of us brought up in the Western world can connect with immediately. For one thing, the dominant view in our culture is that there is just one lifetime, so thinking in terms of endless lifetimes might not come naturally. We also live in a culture where mothers are not always respected and are, in fact, sometimes blamed for the troubles we are having. So here are a few more ways to think about the equality of all beings.

Our Uniqueness

An interesting way to look at the equality of all beings, as taught by the Zen teacher Shunryu Suzuki Roshi, is that everybody is equal because we are all unique. "What?" you might say. "If we're unique, then we're different from one another." That is true, and the very fact that every being is different makes us equal. We are equal in our uniqueness.

We live in an amazing reality. Within the great multiplicity of phenomena, there are no two things alike. The most famous example is snowflakes. Of the billions of snowflakes that fall each year, there are never two that are identical. Each snowflake is completely unique. Each blade of grass, each flower, and each cloud in the sky is unique. A mother in a large herd of antelope can find her child because it is unique. Each person is also unique. Of course, some people are more alike than others, but there are no two people who are absolutely identical—not even identical twins.

The first Buddhist teaching that really stopped me in my tracks was a short contemplation from the Tibetan monastic tradition that I read in the 1960s. The name of the book is long since lost to my memory, but the contemplation remains. It has three parts:

> I am not better than anyone else.
> I am not worse than anyone else.
> I am not equal to anyone else.

The last line stopped me because I had always been taught to believe that I was equal to others. I grew up in the United States, where everyone is believed to be equal. Yet this Buddhist contemplation said, "I am not equal to anyone else." There is no comparison, no measurement at all. So it is not a contradiction to say that in our uniqueness, we are all equal.

The Center of the Universe

Another way in which we are equal with all other beings is that each of us perceives ourselves to be the center of the universe. This is an accurate perception. It has nothing to do with selfishness. We each have a body, we are where we are, and everything else revolves around this perspective.

The same is true for every other being in the universe that has a body and sense perceptions. We all perceive ourselves as the center of the world, with everything revolving around us. We are all the same that way.

Birth and Death

All beings are born, and all beings will die. In this way, too, all beings are equal.

The Desire for Happiness

Another quality we share with all other beings is the desire to be happy. Everyone wants to feel fulfilled and satisfied, as though nothing more were needed. We are all equal in this way. We are also equal to one another in not wanting to suffer. All beings do not want to feel pain, and when we experience pain, we all want to get rid of it. We are equal in wanting to be free of suffering.

However, we get confused about what causes happiness and what causes suffering. Not understanding karma, the laws of cause and effect, we do things to try to make ourselves happy but end up causing suffering. Karma is simply the idea that everything we do sets something else in motion, and that motion works according to certain principles. For example, if I throw a pebble into a pond, it will make ripples. That is cause and effect, how things work. A pebble thrown into a pond would never make fire, it always makes ripples.

Likewise, if we steal something because we think that having it is going to make us happy, that is not seeing the bigger picture and pattern. Stealing will always cause suffering—for the person you stole from, to begin with, and eventually for you. Taking what is not offered does not create happiness, any more than a rock thrown into a pond creates fire.

It is an interesting exercise to watch the news and think about how everyone involved in a news story is motivated by the desire for happiness. A man swindles old people out of their life savings because he thinks that retiring to an Italian villa will make him happy. Young people blow themselves up to kill "infidels," believing that such an act of sacrifice will take them to paradise, where they will be happy forever.

Everybody is equal in wanting to be happy, but by not understanding what causes happiness, we continue to cause suffering. Everyone is also equal in wanting to be free from suffering.

Buddha Nature

Another way in which all beings are equal is that we all possess buddha nature. When Buddha realized enlightenment, he clearly perceived that all beings in their essence, in their original nature, are not any different from what he had realized: primordially awake, pure from the beginning. This is called our buddha nature, awake nature, or basic goodness. It pervades all beings equally.

According to Buddhist tradition, beings can be divided into three categories:

1. Those lost in confusion and pain
2. Bodhisattvas on the path of awakening
3. Buddhas

Among these three categories of beings, there is not any difference in buddha nature—the amount and quality is identical. The only difference is that those lost in confusion and pain turn away from buddha nature, bodhisattvas turn toward buddha nature, and buddhas have realized buddha nature. Other than that, there is no difference. All beings are equal in buddha nature.

Bringing It into Our Experience
Rousing the Awakened Mind of Equanimity

We have discussed six ways in which all beings are equal. It is good to contemplate these. In your sitting meditation practice, or when simply sitting quietly, take five minutes or so and ponder these six ways in which we are all equal. Take one at a time and explore its implications. Then move to the next one. When we contemplate how we are equal to all other beings that live on this earth, we are preparing the ground for expanding our love to include them all.

Then contemplate the fourth limitless aspiration for a moment: "May all beings dwell in the great equanimity free from passion, aggression, and prejudice." In making this wish, we are wishing for a world at peace. This is our first exercise in thinking bigger. Feel this aspiration in your heart, then let the thoughts go and return to the present moment with the breath.

You can also think about one or all six of these at any time. They help us to cultivate a realistic and healthy perspective.

All beings are equal in the following ways:

1. They have at some time been our mothers.
2. They are unique.
3. They perceive themselves as the center of the universe.
4. They are born and will die.
5. They want to be happy and free from suffering.
6. They all possess buddha nature.

May all beings dwell in the great equanimity free from passion, aggression, and prejudice.

LOVE

May all beings enjoy happiness and the root of happiness.

Let's turn now to the first of the Four Limitless Ones: love. In the Buddhist tradition, love is expressed as the wish for the happiness of others. Why is it expressed this way? Why not wish for love itself? As we have discussed, *love* is a very complicated word, with many different meanings and innuendos. Love can also become very neurotic and can involve projecting all kinds of fantasies onto others. But one quality that real love always has is the desire for the loved one to be happy. I cannot think of any situation in which this is not true. No matter how confused love might become, somewhere deep down there is a genuine wish for your loved one to be happy. So here love is expressed, "May all beings enjoy happiness and the root of happiness."

What we mean by "enjoy[ing] happiness" is getting what you want, like a car, a relationship, a job, or a good situation in your life. You feel fulfilled; another way of saying it is that you're in a state of not needing so much. We wish that for all beings.

The "root of happiness" is a connection to basic goodness. The conditions that cause happiness in the world will always change, and worldly happiness will be lost, just as clouds change in the sky. True and lasting happiness can come only from within, from a mind that is at peace and awake. One can develop such a mind by rousing the thought, the wish, and the aspiration that all beings could enjoy happiness and the root of happiness.

As is always the case in Buddhist practice, we are not trying to create something new or better, we are trying to bring out what is already here, already within us. We have all experienced love and wanted our loved ones to be happy. In this practice of rousing bodhichitta, awakened heart and mind, we are taking the love we already feel and making it bigger.

Bringing It into Our Experience
Rousing the Awakened Mind of Love in Seven Steps

As you read each step, think about the words, feel them, and let them take your mind on a journey.

1. We can start with ourselves. We can wish for our own happiness. We can make a gesture of friendship to ourself. Contemplate your own happiness for a minute. What is happiness?

2. Think of someone you love, then think of a time your loved one was happy and how his or her happiness made you feel. Let your mind stay with that feeling for a moment.

3. Take that feeling of love and expand it to include your family and friends.

4. Imagine expanding this love to include the people you pass on the street, the people you stand with in a checkout line, anywhere and everywhere. You don't particularly know them other than to say hello, perhaps. These are people you

feel neutral about. They are the people who live in your town or your neighborhood. Rouse the aspiration that they could enjoy happiness today. Expand your love to them.

5. Expand this feeling of love to someone you consider an enemy. Rouse the wish that your enemy be happy. This step is generally the most challenging.

6. Dissolve the boundaries by contemplating everyone you have thought of thus far: "May I, my loved ones, my acquaintances, and my enemies enjoy happiness and the root of happiness."

7. Expand your love to all beings on earth. Cultivate your love by wishing that they all enjoy happiness.

When you are finished, let your mind relax and rest in the present moment with the breath.

Simple but Profound

The practice of wishing happiness to others is so simple that it is easy to overlook its profundity. This is a contemplation practice. It uses words and thoughts to take the mind and heart on a journey. It is like an exercise to strengthen the muscle of the mind, to make it more flexible and open. First, we think about the words "May all beings be happy." The words point us toward the meaning of love, so our minds and our hearts go in that direction. As we become familiar with this new, bigger meaning, we can let the words go and rest in that meaning—love includes wishing happiness for others.

Sometimes these contemplations touch us emotionally, and sometimes they are just thoughts. It doesn't matter. If you work with this contemplation over time, you will find that your experience is different at different times, but each time that you think, "May all beings be happy," you are planting that aspiration in your consciousness as a seed, and it becomes the motivation to act in ways that will bring happiness to beings and free them from suffering.

Someone might ask, "Is it really possible for everyone to be happy? Can both the hunter and the prey get what they want? By rousing this aspiration that everyone be happy, aren't we just butting our heads against a wall?" The answer is no, we aren't. From a Buddhist perspective, we can aspire for the happiness of both the hunter and the prey and plant that love deep in our hearts. Remember, this is a practice of aspiration. If we get caught up in the logistics or the practicalities, we might miss that crucial point. If one day a genie appears from inside a bottle and grants us one wish, there would be no hesitation: "May all beings be happy."

Of course, rousing the mind of love is an exercise in imagination. We are using our imagination to expand our heart and mind to include all beings in our love by wishing them happiness. In reality, we might be far from actually feeling that, but trying to imagine it provides a way to touch that vision of love and opens our hearts and minds. It provides a new direction, a path, a way to proceed.

When we do this practice, we will probably discover that there are people whom we don't want to be happy. We find that we cannot wish this person or these people happiness. We just can't do it. We have run into the boundary beyond which our love cannot go. In this way, the practice of rousing bodhichitta not only plants seeds of love in our mind; just as important, it also helps us to become more self-aware. We meet our limits. That is okay. We are not saints. If we continue, we are doing two things: we are stretching our boundaries, making them more pliable, and we are waking up and becoming more aware of our own mind.

Here's a personal story along these lines. I was first taught the practice of rousing bodhichitta by my teacher Sakyong Mipham at a three-month meditation and study retreat. Several times a day, we wished

"May all beings be happy" as part of our meditation. Before each talk, Sakyong Mipham led us in a guided meditation on "May all beings be happy." For three months I roused this wish and aspiration several times every day.

On the way home, my eleven-year-old daughter, Cecily, and I were sitting in the Denver airport, waiting to board our plane. Hundreds of people passed by every few minutes. As I sat there and watched, the thought arose from habit, "May all beings be happy." I realized with a shock that I did not really want these people to be happy. I thought I knew more than they did and was living my life in a better way. Actually, I almost wanted them to suffer the consequences of what I saw as their blind materialism.

I was astonished at myself. After three months of wishing happiness to all beings, I saw very clearly that I did not really want the people right in front of me to be happy. It was as though someone had turned on the lights inside my mind. I could see that rather than being full of love, my mind was full of arrogance.

At one time in my youth I had thought that I might attain enlightenment in this lifetime. Sitting there in the Denver airport, looking at all those people and seeing my own mind, I realized that if I could cultivate just a little bit more love and compassion in this life, that would be really good. Don't worry about enlight-enment, I told myself. If I could travel even just a little bit further on the path of the bodhisattva by generat-ing a little more love and compassion for others in my being, that would be a life well lived. This is when I started taking this simple practice of wishing happiness for others seriously. When we become more aware of ourselves, we don't always see what we want to see, but that is how we learn and set ourselves in a new direction.

Part of the simplicity of the practice is that you can wish beings happiness anywhere, anytime. We have looked at the longer, formal way of rousing love. Tak-ing our time and expanding step-by-step helps us to actually experience and become familiar with the process. But it also works to simply think, "May all be-ings be happy" or even just "May these beings be happy" or "May this being be happy." We can use one of these thoughts as a simple object of contemplation at times of reflection or anytime during the day.

Maybe your morning is rushed. You are on your way to work, sitting in the subway, on a bus, or in your car. You could take a few minutes to wish, "May all beings be happy today" or "May all these people on this bus enjoy happiness today." You are going to be thinking, anyway, so why not spend a few minutes thinking a thought that will change the world, that will bring yourself and others happiness now and in the future? Please try it.

It's like having a little Buddha sitting on your shoulder. You whisper to him, "If I want to travel on the path of awakening, what should I think about?" And the Buddha whispers in your ear, "Think, 'May all beings be happy.'"

So any time is a good time to wish happiness for others: during a wedding, at a funeral, when you are happy, when you can't sleep, when you are depressed. Walking into a business meeting, you have an agenda you need to accomplish, yet you can still rouse the wish that everyone in the meeting enjoy happiness in their lives. Rousing a mind like that naturally creates a good society.

COMPASSION

May all beings be free from suffering and the root of suffering.

Compassion is expressed as the wish for freedom from suffering. Compassion is a form of love, but here the emphasis is on responding to the suffering of beings and wishing that it be removed. Sometimes thinking about love (wishing happiness) is appropriate; at other times it is more appropriate to think about compassion (freedom from suffering). It is good to cultivate both of them, for they go hand in hand.

By "suffering" we mean pain that is brought on by causes and conditions such as sickness, difficult relationships, accidents, loss, anxiety, and so forth. We aspire that all beings—and you should always remember that "all beings" includes you—be free from pain and liberated from suffering. What a big thought!

Being liberated from the "root of suffering" means seeing that this separate thing I call "me" has never really been separate from the rest of existence. The Buddha discovered that the illusion of a separate self has led to all the unhappiness, cruelty, hatred, and violence in the world. Once we see this, too, we can choose to let go of ego and rest in our basic goodness.

Bringing It into Our Experience
Rousing the Awakened Mind of Compassion in Seven Steps

1. Contemplate your own desire to be free from pain and suffering.
2. Think of someone you love and a time when that loved one was suffering, so your heart naturally goes out to this person and you wish you could take the suffering away. Stay with that feeling for a minute.

THE POWER OF A WISH

3. Take that feeling of compassion and expand it
   to include your family and friends.
4. Expand your compassion, the wish that beings
   be free from suffering, to include the neutral
   people you meet in your day-to-day life.
5. Rouse the wish that your enemy be free from
   suffering.
6. Dissolve the boundaries by contemplating
   everyone you have thought of thus far: "May
   I, my loved ones, my acquaintances, and my
   enemies be free from suffering and the root
   of suffering."
7. Expand your compassion to all beings on earth.
   Cultivate your compassion by wishing that they
   could all be free from suffering.

At the end, let your mind relax and rest in the
present moment with the breath.

JOY

*May all beings not be separated from the great happiness devoid
of suffering.*

This aspiration describes joy, which is not the same as
regular happiness. Happiness arises from the coming

together of certain conditions—for example, you have a good job and are in a satisfying relationship and so you are happy. But then one of those conditions changes—for example, the relationship falls apart and so you are unhappy. What we generally refer to as happiness occurs through the coming together of particular circumstances. However, everything in life changes. There are sunny days and rainy days. Happiness comes and goes.

"The great happiness devoid of suffering" refers to a happiness that doesn't turn into its opposite. This is joy. Joy is not so much based on conditions but is more fundamental. It is unconditional happiness.

Joy and love are closely related. Sometimes in a relationship—such as when you first fall in love or when your baby or your grandchild is born—it is so clear that love and joy are inseparable. You experience love, you experience joy; you experience joy, you are in love.

By cultivating love in our heart and mind by aspiring that all beings be happy, we are expanding the potential for joy. We can fulfill that potential by rousing the awakened mind in its expression as joy for the happiness of others. This is called *sympathetic joy*. When others experience happiness and success, we nurture feelings of sympathetic joy for their happiness and success. We cultivate the feeling of great happiness for them, which is joy, the consummation of love.

Like cultivating love by wishing all beings happiness, rejoicing in the happiness of others is easiest when the other person is someone close to us. Joy often arises naturally when we see happiness in someone we love. It becomes more challenging as the object of our joy is further away from us and our inner circle of family and friends.

When we are cultivating joy, we discover our limits in the form of feelings of envy and jealousy, which are the opposite of sympathetic joy. I want to emphasize, though, that having feelings such as envy and jealousy is not bad, per se. We do not need to try to get rid of them. They arise on their own in our minds. We don't have to think badly of ourselves because of it. The most important thing is that we become aware of these feelings. We could learn to see them for what they are: part of ego's games. When we have that awareness, we can plant the seed of joy and rouse sympathetic joy by thinking, "I feel joy for their happiness and success."

Like cultivating love and compassion, cultivating joy for others' happiness also illuminates what's in our mind. Arousing sympathetic joy is like holding a highly polished mirror up to our mind. In my practice I become aware of even a tiny amount of envy, the feeling that another's gain or success should be mine, because I have noticed that whenever I am comparing myself to someone else, there can be no joy.

With awareness, we can shift our allegiance from ego's games to basic goodness. We can notice an envious thought, and we know where it will lead. Let's think about it. When we feel envy for someone else's possessions, qualities, or luck, we are discontented and resentful. There is an aggrieved longing or desire for it to be ours. That is how envy makes us feel. If we let that fester, we will become bitter, and this bitterness will wait in ambush for an opportunity to express its anger and cause pain to others. Is that the seed we want to plant in our garden?

If we are aware of an envious thought toward someone and can say to ourselves, with a sense of humor, "I am green with envy at your success," then we can begin to transform the negative consequences of envy into something more positive—turning the envy into a compliment and maybe a smile. Beyond that, we can plant a seed of joy by cultivating sympathetic joy. We can use our imaginations and rouse the thought "I feel joy for your success." In these ways, we can gradually shift our allegiance from envy to joy and love.

Bringing It into Our Experience
Rousing the Awakened Mind of Sympathetic Joy

Bring to mind people who are happy and cultivate the feeling of joy for their happiness. Whenever you hear of some one else's success and happiness, arouse sympathetic joy for that person.

The experience of joy is a flow of free energy, life energy. Joy comes from being present and expanding our love and compassion. This releases energy that is otherwise caught in the grip of maintaining ego's games. When all of our energy is involved in maintaining our ego, our energy cannot flow. It is constantly bouncing back and forth—"What about me? How am I doing?"—over and over, all the time. Our energy has become captive to our little minds.

When we rouse a bigger heart and mind, when we slowly, step-by-step, day by day, expand our love and compassion based on seeing the equality of all beings, we massage and soften those boundaries, and soon the energy that has been usurped by ego is freed and can flow. That flow of free energy is joy.

Joy is more fundamental than happiness because it doesn't arise from ego and what it wants. Joy arises from love, and love takes us beyond the ego, beyond preoccupation with the self, to place the welfare of others first. Happiness is generally mostly about me, but joy is always bigger than me.

True Bravery

HOW DOES A BODHISATTVA manifest this love beyond ego—beyond our preoccupations with our personal happiness—in our everyday lives? By using what the Buddhist tradition calls the six far-gone actions. "Far-gone action" is one way that my teacher Chögyam Trungpa translated the Sanskrit word *paramita,* which literally means "from the other shore." It refers to action that does not arise from ego, from "What about me?" (which is "this shore"). Paramita is action that comes from a different perspective, an open and awake mind and heart.

GENEROSITY

The first far-gone action is generosity. The Buddhist teachings encourage many types of generosity, such as giving a person a material thing that he needs, be it food or an iPhone. Another type of generosity is helping a person through a difficult time, being there for her. Anytime you give something to others, it is almost always good.

An essential quality of the far-gone aspect of generosity is opening to and welcoming others as they are. We discussed this in some detail earlier: flashing generosity to your partner or your child, seeing your loved ones in a fresh way in the present moment. We broke down this flash into steps: contacting warmth in ourselves, expanding the warmth outward, and melting our fixed ideas so that we see others as they are, even if only for a brief moment, rather than seeing our opinions of them. This glimpse of openness is bodhichitta, the awakened heart and mind that naturally possess the qualities of warmth and clarity. It is a little leap beyond our usual ways of doing things into the space of openness—the natural, clear, and uncluttered aspect of our being. If our wish is for others to be happy, the expression of that is opening to and welcoming others as they are. The bodhisattva path, the journey of awakening, is composed of many little leaps into openness.

Please don't misunderstand the word *opening*. It does not mean that we have license to act out, to say or do anything, or to be impulsive and call that "being open." We are not using the word in that way at all. We are using it more in the sense of opening the shutter of a camera so that the light can get in, or like a flower opening to the sun.

Opening requires personal bravery. The bodhisattva path is one of opening to yourself, others, and the world, and opening is a courageous thing to do. The very nature of opening means that you don't know exactly what you will find or what it will bring. Opening requires a little leap. Therefore, it is traditional to speak of a *warrior bodhisattva*, with *warrior* meaning "one who is brave." It takes a lot of bravery just to open to yourself and be your own best friend. When you take that first posture of bravery, gentleness, and strength— "I am here. I feel the way I do"—with kindness and warmth, the path unfolds from that courage.

When you flash the far-gone action of generosity to your partner, child, friend, colleague, or perhaps even to your enemy, you are opening without expectation, welcoming these people as they are. You are also cultivating the clarity and warmth of openness. You are learning to open and to trust in that. You are developing the trust that you can just *be* and that your being is already basic goodness. The path of the warrior bodhisattva is to cultivate confidence, step-by-step, in opening and letting go into the energy of basic goodness.

If you've ever had a broken heart, then you know ways to protect your heart. We all have our defenses, our ways of warding off being touched and being hurt. We might well have layers and layers of defenses and fortifications. The bravery of the bodhisattva lies in the willingness, indeed, the commitment, to open the heart, to not close and protect it.

When we flash generosity to another person, cutting the chain reaction of karma, we are stepping out into the open. The far-gone part is that we are stepping out with no expectations of benefit or reward. There are no strings attached. We are simply opening.

This flash of generosity, this opening outward, or glimpse of bodhichitta ignites further potential. The question becomes how to cultivate confidence in opening to basic goodness so that it becomes part of who we are rather than just a flash. This journey of gaining confidence in openness is described in the rest of the six far-gone actions, but nothing can unfold without the first flash of awakening in the far-gone action of generosity.

Generosity is opening to and welcoming others, the first gesture of a bodhisattva.

DISCIPLINE

We are not accustomed to being out in the open without our habitual opinions and patterns, so the natural tendency when we find ourselves there is to close in and reestablish a fortress of protection around ourselves. Understanding this, the Buddha gave us the second far-gone action: discipline.

Discipline, in this case, doesn't mean imposing something on ourselves but rather relating to the fact that we are already present. Discipline is self-existing, from that point of view. Discipline could be described as "taking your seat" in the open space of generosity. Or if you are standing, feeling your feet on the ground, be it the earth, the floor, or the sidewalk. By relating to earth and being present, you are able to remain in open awareness longer.

There are two basic principles the warrior bodhisattva

cultivates. Being present is the mindfulness principle, and being aware of what is going on within us and around us is the awareness principle.

Mindfulness has a sense of precision and often has an object, something that the mind is focusing on. For example, you could be mindful of the way you are holding this book. You notice all the details involved, the weight of the book, the position of your arms and hands, the texture of the pages and cover on your fingertips. That is mindfulness.

These details take place in a greater space, a bigger situation. This includes how and where you are sitting, the environment around you that you perceive with your sense perceptions—what you see, hear, smell, taste, and touch—and the sensations of your body. This bigger picture is the awareness principle. Chögyam Trungpa used the term *panoramic awareness*. This is 360-degree awareness, or awareness of the totality.

The far-gone action of discipline is to touch the experience of simply being present and aware as a basic reference point of sanity and wakefulness. When you want to retreat from openness and rebuild your fortress, simply touch that experience. Because you are already here, because you are already present and aware, all you have to do is touch it. Taking your seat gently in this way will allow the qualities of opening and openness in the far-gone action of generosity to continue to unfold.

When we do this, we might experience a feeling of awkwardness. We have stepped out of the costume we ordinarily wear (our habitual reactions and patterns), so we might feel slightly naked and exposed. It was very helpful for me when my teacher talked about "awkward spontaneity." If we take a step into openness by flashing generosity and touching earth, we let go of our little bag of tricks, the habitual ways we respond to situations. If we relate with a person openly, in the present moment, even though it might be someone we relate with every day, we have, in fact, never been in this situation before. Not really. When we realize that we have never been in this situation, we free ourselves from a lot of baggage we have been carrying around. We might feel fresh and light, but perhaps awkward, not knowing quite what to do. But because we have never been in this situation before, what we do will naturally be spontaneous. This is awkward spontaneity.

Essentially, the far-gone action of discipline means keeping your feet on the ground.

Discipline means touching the earth because you are already present.

PATIENCE

When we stay open longer, we will experience pain and irritation. This is not because opening itself is painful, but because, realistically speaking, there is a lot of pain that occurs in relationships, family and work situations, and the world in general. By opening, we can become aware of how much pain others are in. Sometimes it may even seem like they are taking advantage of our openness to inflict pain on us. Or maybe they just irritate us. Whatever the source, our natural reaction to experiencing pain and irritation is to close off, to step back into our fortress, to arm ourselves with our weapons. So in order to prolong the openness, the Buddha gave us the third far-gone action: patience.

Patience in this context is not patience in the sense of waiting for something to happen or for something to go away. Patience, like all of the far-gone actions, takes place in the present moment. Patience here means not pushing our experience away, whether it be pleasurable or painful. The discomfort of pain arouses aggression in the sense that we want to push it away. Patience is the opposite of aggression. It is nonaggression, which means experiencing whatever is present and not rejecting it.

A vivid example of how we might apply the far-gone action of patience is in the way we work with anger. (We can apply the same principles we are about to discuss to working with any emotion that afflicts our minds, be it jealousy, lust, greed, fear, or boredom.) Anger is the greatest enemy of the bodhisattva. When it takes hold, it's as though the "dark side" has won.

Anger is destructive, or, more accurately, anger is destruction. It can certainly destroy a relationship. It can destroy a person's heart and mind. It can destroy peace, and it thrives on war. One outburst of anger can undo many kindnesses. Anger generally intends harm, and once the intent to harm is present in the mind, it goes against the bodhisattva's wish that beings enjoy happiness and the intent to always bring benefit to them. That's why anger is the bodhisattva's enemy. How does a bodhisattva practitioner face the enemy of anger without anger? The bodhisattva does this by actually facing the energy of anger itself.

Generally, anger feels uncomfortable and we want to act it out, get rid of it, toss it to someone else like a hot potato. So we quickly find a focus or target for our anger. Here's the bravery of a bodhisattva: rather than directing the anger outward, he or she turns toward the anger. A bodhisattva warrior is willing to experience the energy and texture of the anger very directly, with kindness.

It is said that if a person throws a stick, a dog will always chase the stick, but a lion will go to the person who threw it. As warrior bodhisattvas, we need to be like the lion. Don't try to deflect the anger by directing it to someone else. "It's his fault. It's her fault." That is like the dog chasing the stick. Instead, experience the energy of the anger for yourself, very personally. Like a lion, go to where the anger is coming from. Feel the anger itself without acting on it. This is the far-gone action of patience—opening to our experience as it is. Patience is the opposite of speed and aggression, and it is founded in a fundamental friendship and openness with ourself.

Patience is also founded in understanding karma. Anger is karma in action, so to speak. A situation causes anger, and when anger grips the mind, there is no room for anything else. Expressing anger toward someone else simply exacerbates the situation. Like a forest fire, anger feeds on itself, consuming all the fuel in its path in its onslaught of destruction.

Understanding this, the bodhisattva practitioner learns to catch the anger before it gets out of control. When it is just a little grass fire, we can take definitive action to put it out. Once it's a forest fire, there is little to do but let it burn out and survey the damage.

How do we catch ourselves, and then what do we do

with our anger? We learn to catch ourselves by cultivating mindfulness, training ourselves to come back
to the present moment again and again. This creates
awareness of what is happening in our minds. "I see
that little spark of anger. I can feel that anger smolder-
ing." These little gaps of mindfulness and awareness
begin to open the potential for choosing new alternatives. We know from experience where our habitual
responses will lead us. We can catch this opportunity
and shift our allegiance.

Having caught ourselves and noticed the spark of
anger, what do we do next?

In one way or another, we should give the situation
space rather than fuel. Fuel is like oxygen to a fire;
space is like a vacuum where fire can't ignite. On a
coarse level, this might simply mean removing ourselves from the object of anger, taking some cooling-
off time before we communicate with the other
person. Adding space might also mean making a gesture of friendship to ourselves or a flash of generosity
to the object of our anger, creating a little gap in which
we can see that we have alternatives.

One of these alternatives is to just experience the
energy of the anger itself. When we feel angry, we usually immediately create a story line in our minds

about why we're angry. This story line serves to justify our anger, fuel it, and determine where best to unload it. "Once again he's late, and I can't stand it anymore. He knows how much this bothers me, and he won't make the effort to change. This is so typical of him." The story line that accompanies anger is like wind. Going over and over the story line in our thoughts fans the flames. If we are willing to experience the texture of the anger itself rather than go over and over the story line of why we are angry, we will give the anger space rather than fan the flames.

The bodhisattva practitioner turns toward the anger without anger. In this process, we do not seek to extinguish the anger, but we are curious about it and feel a commitment to living differently, to stepping out of our habitual responses. So we summon the bravery to engage the actual energy of the anger—not the storyline, but the energy itself. Where is it? What does it feel like? Curiosity will give it space, and then our actions can become more skillful. Perhaps we can pacify the anger and bring out the intelligence that is often there underneath it.

If we can get this far, we are doing really well. Catching ourselves is the most important point, because without that awareness, karma (cause and effect) will simply play itself out. If we catch ourselves, we can take definitive action with the intent of bringing benefit rather than harm.

As we travel on the path, we can learn to be more skillful. We can also learn from the times we don't catch ourselves—by looking back, not to prove ourselves right or wrong, but to see when we missed our chance and got hooked in the momentum of the anger (or envy, greed, pride, or any emotion that separates us from others and the awakened state of mind). A warrior bodhisattva doesn't consider getting hooked a failure but an opportunity to learn.

At first our attempts might be awkward and not at all skillful, but we can learn from our successes and our failures. If we can catch ourselves, we can try to create a gap in the karmic momentum. We can open to our experience as it is. Open space is the most powerful weapon of a warrior bodhisattva.

Patience is opening to our experience just as it is.

EXERTION

The far-gone actions of generosity, discipline, and patience are tools that we use, skillful means, actions that we take. After a while, a bodhisattva on the path might get tired or forget and stop using these tools.

Understanding this, the Buddha gave us the fourth far-gone action: exertion.

Exertion is like a little wake-up call. It is not at all like feeling guilty or carrying on out of a sense of duty or religious belief. Here, exertion is a quick reminder: when we shift our allegiance from the alluring safety of habitual responses and patterns to the freshness of generosity, the sanity of discipline, and the realness of patience, it brings joy.

There is still some quality of effort—we have to keep applying the tools of generosity, discipline, and patience. But it's good effort and exertion because it makes sense. A bodhisattva on the path discovers the joyous aspect of applying these tools, of seeing that energy does not have to be forced but that it develops spontaneously as we let go of ego's strategies and games.

As confidence in this grows, the warrior begins to shift allegiance from the alluring comfort of habitual responses and patterns to the freshness of being awake, the delight of discipline, and the energy of patience—the experience of being fully present. This is not a duty but a delight, because one has already established the connection between the action and one's being—between opening, being present and aware, not pushing our experience away, and the experience of being alive and awake in this world.

When you understand why you are doing something, it is easy to exert yourself at the task.

Exertion means finding both good sense and delight in your practice.

MEDITATION

Perhaps a bodhisattva finds that joyous energy exhilarating and inspiring. A student bodhisattva, however, may sometimes feel overwhelmed and discouraged by the suffering in the world. He or she might alternate between these highs and lows. In order to stabilize the openness achieved in the first four paramitas, the Buddha gave us the fifth far-gone action: meditation.

Meditation in this context means not just sitting meditation practice, it also has the sense of getting accustomed to waking up in the present moment. The far-gone action of meditation means becoming accustomed to generosity, to taking your seat, to not pushing your experience away, to exertion, and to joy. Above all, meditation means getting accustomed to openness. In fact, meditation and openness are the very same thing.

As the bodhisattva cultivates stability in the experience of generosity, discipline, patience, and exertion, he or she begins to experience an unconditional confidence in openness. Unconditional confidence does not arise from causes and conditions, such as feeling well prepared. It is based not on becoming something but on being. Like the sun, like basic goodness, unconditional confidence just is. It is the source of the innate bravery of the warrior bodhisattva.

Chögyam Trungpa taught that the far-gone action of meditation is "the means of stabilizing oneself within the framework of seeing relationships, and thereby seeing that one can afford to open. This openness and keen meditative intelligence brings one to deal with the nowness of each new situation."

Meditation is stabilizing open awareness in the present moment.

PRAJNA

Dealing with the nowness of each new situation is the fruit of the five far-gone actions, or skillful means, of generosity, discipline, patience, exertion, and meditation. The sixth far-gone action, *prajna,* is the wisdom that is realized from nowness.

If there were a good translation of the word *prajna,* I would not use the Sanskrit word. *Prajna* literally means "the best way of knowing." What is the best way to know? Directly. We are not talking about accumulating knowledge from books or the Internet. We are talking about the direct knowing that can occur only in the present moment, within nowness.

We have a connection with reality even before we think. This natural, self-existing connection can wake us up and make us feel fundamentally good. This is the discovery of basic goodness.

The word *prajna* refers to a direct experience that is somewhat muted by the English word *knowing*, which implies that there is a separation, a kind of buffer or duality, between the knower and that which is known. In order to not lose the quality of direct experience, many Buddhist teachers simply use the word *prajna*. Over time it will become part of the English language, like the word *karma*, because it doesn't have a direct translation.

As with basic goodness, in cultivating prajna we are not making something up or creating something that is not already here. In trying to understand what prajna is, it might be good to use an example on a very ordinary level: It is prajna that allows children to learn how to tie their shoes. Children have to have clarity to be able to perceive what is happening. They need precision in order to hold the laces correctly and make the little loop. They have to have intelligence to remember the whole process. They are learning something new, but the natural ability to learn is self-existing, already present.

On the bodhisattva path, that self-existing, clear, precise, and intelligent state of knowing called prajna is cultivated, brought out, cleaned up, and sharpened, so to speak. All of the skillful means, such as sitting meditation and flashing generosity, have an element of cultivating and bringing out this clear, precise, and intelligent state of being.

When we can relax into the simplicity of sitting meditation practice, just sitting and breathing, that simplicity has a sharp quality that penetrates the complexity of our confusion and lays bare a vivid experience of sitting and breathing in the present moment.

When we flash generosity and melt our fixed ideas and opinions, there is an instant of clarity that is natural and uncluttered. This allows us to perceive in a much clearer way than perceiving through the web of our generalizations and opinions. We can know the situation as it is in the present moment. That is awakening our natural intelligence by opening. One general translation we could use for *prajna* is "wakefulness."

Prajna is an important tool on the bodhisattva path that we can use to see through our own limited versions of reality and discover the true nature of things.

Prajna sees the potential of egolessness. When prajna sees through ego's games, it reveals openness—the natural, clear, and uncluttered ground that is basic goodness.

Prajna knows basic goodness—natural, clear, and uncluttered.

The six far-gone actions, or paramitas, describe a journey of opening and gaining confidence in basic goodness. One doesn't have to look elsewhere or in some other time. The journey of a warrior bodhisattva is about awakening to the magic of each moment. The path of awakening is a lifelong journey, and it always takes place right in the middle of our lives.

When my wife and I were married in a Buddhist wedding ceremony, the vow we took was to relate to each other and to the world according to the six far-gone actions: generosity, discipline, patience, exertion (joy), meditation, and prajna. They have proved to be trustworthy and beneficial. They contain enormous wisdom on how to contribute to a stable and creative relationship, deepen love for each other, and cultivate unending friendship, and they provide the practical tools for applying this wisdom in our day-to-day lives.

The path of the warrior bodhisattva starts at home with a flash of generosity to our partners, children, friends, neighbors, and coworkers. We can always wake up in the middle of any situation. When we wake up, we see more clearly, beyond our own preoccupations, and we perceive what is needed. We can be more generous, take our seats, not push our experience away, enjoy exertion, and become familiar with open awareness. This brings more prajna, more wisdom. Skillful means and wisdom support each other, from the first flash of generosity throughout the journey of opening and openness.

There is no rush. The love of a bodhisattva, of an awake being, is an ongoing journey that expresses itself moment to moment in our everyday lives in how we treat ourselves, our loved ones, our neighbors, our enemies, all beings on earth, and the earth itself.

Love and Loyalty

WHETHER WE ARE talking about loving a partner, a child, a friend, or all beings on earth for all time, if there is no loyalty, our love has no substance. It is like a hollow tree that will easily be blown over by the winds of karma. Love with loyalty is like a strong tree that can move with the wind but will not break.

Ever since my daughter was a little girl, when she says good night or good-bye to me, she has said, "Love and loyalty." (Sometimes we hold up a thumb and an index finger in the shape of an *L* to each other, for *love* and *loyalty*.) When she became a young adult, I asked her why she had added *loyalty* to *love*, and she said to me, "Love can be a very emotional, like an almost uncontrollable feeling you have for someone. When you add the word *loyalty* to *love*, it turns it into something different. It becomes more like a way of life."

As we approach the end of this little book, let's explore the notion of loyalty as love's companion. When we first hear the word *loyalty* in this context, we might think of loyalty to one's spouse, lover, partner, or friend. Loyalty in this sense means not giving the other person any reason to mistrust you. The specifics of this can vary greatly in different relationships, depending on individual and cultural circumstances. What one couple or culture considers loyal, another might consider a betrayal.

Regardless of what it entails, loyalty is an issue in any long-term relationship. Relationships are often tested, at some point, over the issue and definition of loyalty. Each couple or friendship must define the boundaries of the relationship. Loyalty is then based on respecting these definitions and boundaries, and this is what is considered being true to the relationship. This loyalty or its absence will have very much to do with how the relationship unfolds.

Loyalty is generally considered to be an admirable quality in a human being, but whether the results of your loyalty will be beneficial depends on what or whom you are loyal to. For example, loyalty to an abusive relationship will not bring benefit but will only continue the cycle of abuse and dependence. Although this loyalty might feel like an aspect of love, in this case it is misplaced loyalty. It is not helpful but harmful.

Another example is loyalty to a religious or an ideological view that makes you small-minded, rigid, and intolerant of others. Such loyalty is poisoned by arrogance—you are right and everyone else is wrong. Whenever loyalty to something makes you close-minded and close-hearted, it is not beneficial.

If loyalty is a quality worth cultivating, what is trustworthy and beneficial to have loyalty to? According to the teachings of the Buddha, three trustworthy and beneficial objects of loyalty are gentleness, openness, and wisdom. Before we explore those, let's try to understand a little more about the teachings surrounding ego and egolessness.

BEING VERSUS BECOMING

All of the teachings of the Buddha are about *being* rather than *becoming.* They are about uncovering who we most deeply are, rather than about becoming someone new or different. The Buddhist teachings are also based on the realization of egolessness, which simultaneously brings insight and understanding of what ego is and how it operates. The path of the bodhisattva is an egoless journey. Let's explore what egolessness is and is not.

A common misconception is that if someone doesn't have an ego, there would be nobody home—no personality, no spark, no fun. But it is a mistake to equate the Buddhist concept of ego with someone's unique personhood. An egoless person is someone who is authentically present in whatever he or she does—because he or she is not trying to hide anything.

The ego is extra. Ego is the experience that there is a "me" that is completely separate from "everything else." In this scenario, "me" is usually more important. That is our everyday experience, and we base our lives on this perception and assumption. The Buddha, the one who woke up, discovered that this seeming separation never truly existed. It is a misconception based on a slight misperception.

Albert Einstein described this sense of being separate from the rest of the universe as an "optical delusion of consciousness." This is a very accurate description of the Buddhist understanding of ego. It does seem that there is someone "in here" because there is everything else "out there." The perception that we are at the center of the universe is accurate, as we have discussed, but the assumption that we are therefore separate from (and more important than) everything else is an "optical delusion."

Ego's game is to always try to solidify this delusion of separateness into something real. This process is described in Buddhist texts as the *wheel of becoming*. Ego has to constantly become something, since in itself it has no true existence. A slight misperception creates the assumption that "I am separate," and then a whole chain of events is set in motion to solidify our separateness by becoming.

We experience ego's momentum of becoming when we compare our life with an image of what we think it should be. Sometimes we are pleased with ourselves. Sometimes we are displeased. In either case, there is a measuring stick that came from somewhere—an image we compare ourselves to, try to change into, live up to, become.

If you realize egolessness, you have not gotten rid of something real called "ego," but you have seen through ego's games and realized that ego was never actually there to begin with. There is nothing to get rid of, really. It is more a matter of seeing clearly. A traditional analogy for this is walking into a dimly lit room and seeing a snake coiled in the corner, ready to strike. You are filled with fear. Staying as far away from the snake as you can, you edge along the wall, your heart pounding, until you can reach the light switch. You turn on the light and immediately see that it isn't a snake at all, but a coil of rope. All of your fear, so real when you perceived a snake, dissolves instantly, because the snake was never there to begin with. The realization of egolessness is something like that.

Another word for egolessness is *interconnectedness*. We are each unique individuals, but we are interconnected in perceivable and inconceivable ways. The Vietnamese Zen Buddhist teacher Thich Nhat Hanh skillfully uses the word *interbeing* in his teaching to express our interconnectedness. A more technical term would be *interdependent arising*. A flower doesn't blossom in a vacuum; it needs soil, sun, air, and water. When all these conditions are present, a flower blossoms. If any one of them is missing, a flower will not blossom.

A flower appears to be a separate thing. It is beautiful, it smells wonderful, and we can thoroughly appreciate it for what it is. But with greater awareness and deeper thinking, we ultimately cannot separate the flower from the sun and the rain, which cannot be separated from the warmth and the wind, which cannot be separated from the earth and the oceans, which cannot be separated from the trees and the atmosphere, which cannot be separated from you and me. Just as a flower doesn't just blossom in a vacuum, nothing arises on its own. Everything is interconnected in perceivable and inconceivable ways.

Now let's look again at what Einstein said about the delusion of separateness:

> A human being is part of the whole called by us the "universe," a part limited in time and space. We experience our selves, our thoughts, and feelings as something separate from the rest—a kind of optical delusion of consciousness. This delusion is a kind of prison for us, restricting us to our personal desires and affection for a few persons nearest to us. Our task must be to free ourselves from the prison by widening our circle of compassion to embrace all living creatures and the whole of nature in its beauty. The true value of a human being is determined by the measure and the sense in which they have obtained liberation from the self [i.e., ego]. We shall require a substantially new manner of thinking if humanity is to survive.

When we walk on the path of ego or self, we separate ourselves from the world we live in. When we walk on the path of egolessness, our feet can actually touch the ground. Ego, in essence, is the experience of never being present, whereas egolessness brings the experience of being fully present in the moment. Because ego is based on becoming, it always wants something. Egolessness is based on being, and it brings happiness and peace. Ego tends to make us judgmental and hard on ourselves. This is the opposite of the approach of egolessness, which is based on being kind to ourselves as we are. Ego is based on a fundamental deception, a deep level of pretense. Egolessness is genuine and true.

To be genuine and true is to be loyal. It can become a way of life, a way of caring for yourself and all other beings. Being genuine and true is the way of the warrior bodhisattva traveling on the path of egolessness. This path unfolds as gentleness, openness, and wisdom.

LOYALTY TO GENTLENESS

Chögyam Trungpa said, "We can have loyalty to our own gentleness, rather than feeling that we have to run, hide, or produce a better weapon." He is suggesting that we can shift our allegiance from the fight-or-flight response to gentleness. Fight-or-flight is the basic animal instinct of an ego faced with danger: some will stand and fight, and some will run and hide. We commonly do this in our relationships. When you and your partner are in a conflict, do you attack or withdraw? Chögyam Trungpa is pointing out that there is another alternative. If we ever hope to have a peaceful world free of poverty, we as human beings surely have to rise above that level of animal instinct and have greater awareness and love. That is our gift and our responsibility. We can shift our allegiance from the path of ego to the path of egolessness. We can have loyalty to our own gentleness.

As an object of loyalty, gentleness is trustworthy because gentleness has never caused harm to anyone. I should mention that my wife has come up with one example of gentleness possibly doing harm: if you are gentle to a wild animal when it is young, and it gets used to being around people, that could cause problems in the future. There might be other examples, but certainly for the most part, gentleness does not cause harm. And that is where we begin if we want to help our troubled world; we avoid harming other beings.

Gentleness, it must be emphasized, has nothing to do with weakness. Gentleness can have tremendous strength. We could even say that gentleness is the strength of the warrior bodhisattva. It is beneficial to have loyalty to gentleness precisely *because* it is an inexhaustible source of strength (as well as wakefulness). If you can be gentle, if you can find gentleness in the midst of your day, your speed, your preoccupation, your anger, your depression, your happiness, your inspiration, then you will find strength and wakefulness without even looking for them.

Gentleness is the key to opening the treasury of bodhichitta. It opens the doorway of friendship with ourself, which then opens us to others and the world around us. Gentleness does not feel weak, but strong and genuine. It allows us to touch what is true. "I am alive. I am here. I feel the way I do. I am awake." Being gentle with ourself is the opposite of being hard on ourself, and if we are not struggling so much with who we are, we have created some peace and can be more present. Not having to become something, not having to fool anyone, we can be genuine and true. We can be right here, open and available to life.

LOYALTY TO OPENNESS

If we think of gentleness as the ground on which a bodhisattva takes his or her journey, the essential quality of the path itself is opening. This opening is not like trying to open a box from outside to see what's inside. Rather, this opening comes from inside, within the heart and mind. Like love, opening is a journey outward, and it connects the warrior with the energy of basic goodness.

When we are in love, our hearts are naturally open to our loved one, and we are energized and feel fully alive. Our minds are also open to them, which is to say that they are always on our mind. We naturally want them to be happy and free of suffering, and we naturally feel sympathetic joy when they succeed.

The intention of thinking deeply about the Four Limitless Ones is to open our minds and hearts beyond a few people nearest to us, to expand the circle of our love and compassion. The bravery of the warrior bodhisattva is to open and welcome others so that communication can be genuine and true. Simply speaking, gaining confidence in opening is the essence of the path of a warrior bodhisattva.

This confidence has to come from personal experience, from within. We can discover and expand the confidence so that we can open and be fully present, alive, and awake. This is another way of saying that we have confidence in our innate basic goodness, the natural, clear, and uncluttered state of our being. This kind of confidence develops gradually and naturally when we cultivate bodhichitta.

Why is openness trustworthy? Because in itself,

openness is not a thing. It is not something that you can find somewhere. You can shoot an arrow at openness, but there is nothing to puncture. Openness is a way of being. Although it is inherently in us all the time, openness, as we have been using the word, is not naive but highly intelligent because it contains prajna. It is not something that can be possessed, manipulated, or turned into dogma. This is why openness is trustworthy.

It is beneficial to have loyalty to openness because it provides the clear warm space in which people can grow, relationships can deepen, and love can manifest. The openness of an awakened heart and mind is an expression of love. The love of a bodhisattva, however, is not exclusive. Bodhichitta has the intent to benefit all beings on this earth, and for that reason it is immeasurably beneficial to have loyalty to openness.

Loyalty to openness expresses itself in our lives as the intent to move in the direction of openness. Whenever we see that we are stuck in fixed ideas, we can nudge ourselves a little toward openness. For example, perhaps we have been taught to be prejudiced against a certain people because of their ethnicity, religion, sexual orientation, or some other factor. We have closed our hearts to them. If we become aware of this, we can nudge ourselves toward being a little more open-minded and openhearted. We can at least listen and learn. We will have our own point of view, as we should, but our point of view could contain openness to the ideas and customs of others, which would save us all from getting stuck in fixed ideas. Can you imagine a world in which people are not stuck in fixed ideas? Be intelligently open-minded. We can pass that on to our children, our friends, our colleagues, and by doing so we will change the world in big and small ways.

Another opening that occurs on the path of a warrior bodhisattva is opening our awareness through our sense organs: our eyes, ears, nose, tongue, and skin. It is through these gateways that we perceive the world and can form a direct relationship with it. If you are present, you don't have to try to be aware. Awareness is already here, so we can relax and open out into our awareness. When we sit down at work, in a restaurant, or in front of the television, we can make a gesture of friendship to ourself, and from that seat our awareness can open and expand all around. Don't look for something, just see where you are. An accomplished warrior always knows where he or she is and is sensitive to the environment. Student warriors cultivate these qualities gradually on the path.

As we've seen, the journey of opening outward connects the warrior with the energy of basic goodness. How is this so? Because the natural, clear, and uncluttered state of our being is always present, self-existing, and beyond any circumstance. Because basic goodness already is what is, it is not something we can find someplace else. We can find it only by opening fully to the present moment.

In the Shambhala Buddhist tradition, this energy of basic goodness is called *windhorse*. *Wind* refers to our life-force energy, and *horse* refers to the principle of riding energy. Sakyong Mipham defines windhorse as "the ability to ride the inherent strength and vitality of our awareness." Rather than feeling as though our lives are riding us, we can mount and ride the energy and awareness of the present moment. That is always possible. All of the teachings on bodhichitta open us to this richness and provide a way, a path on which to cultivate and uncover confidence in our ability to ride the energy of nowness.

When we open, we automatically contact the energy of windhorse, and we naturally let go of worrying about our own state of mind and begin to think of others. Thus, the intention to benefit others, which gave birth to the warrior bodhisattva, begins to manifest naturally and spontaneously.

LOYALTY TO WISDOM

Gentleness cultivates openness, and openness provides access to the energy of basic goodness, but openness in itself is not enough. We need to know how to
make decisions. We need to have some direction in
our lives, a reference point for deciding to do one thing
and not another. We need wisdom.

We make hundreds of decisions every day. Decisions are such a part of the fabric of our lives that we
are often not even aware that we are making them:
what we say to our partners in the morning and how
we say it, whether we hold a grudge or flash generosity; the tone of voice we use with our children; the
way we treat the people we work with; the way we
treat ourselves. Every decision we make, although it
may seem little and insignificant, has repercussions
for the future.

A bodhisattva on the path of opening becomes a
student of cause and effect. "What are the results of
my actions? Of the words I say? Do they make people
happy or cause confusion? Do they bring benefit or
cause harm?" By cultivating awareness of our actions
and their results in this way, we cultivate discernment. *Discernment* means the ability to make good judg-
ments. With discernment, we can see that there are

121

always alternatives, that we can learn from the past to be more skillful in the present. That sudden space of mindfulness and awareness that allows discernment, rather than habitual responses, leads to wisdom. Sakyong Mipham writes, "Wisdom and compassion begin with cultivating discernment—not just reacting to what happens."

Buddhist tradition teaches us that a bodhisattva chooses speech and actions that possess virtue. It is important to understand this, but we have to be very careful with the word *virtue*. It is heavy with meanings and associations. We are not talking about Victorian virtue. We are not talking at all about virtue that is based on a notion of morality, but virtue that is based on practicality. How can we cultivate situations that will bring happiness and fulfillment to ourselves and others? The answer is quite simple: by being more in tune with our true nature.

Virtue can be defined as thought, speech, and action that is in tune with our true nature, our basic goodness, whereas nonvirtue is out of tune. An action that contains qualities of clarity and warmth, such as the tender way we touch a loved one's cheek, is in tune with basic goodness, and therefore the karmic result will be happiness and love. A nonvirtuous action, in contrast, is not aligned with our basic goodness, which has been obscured by self-absorption. Perhaps anger has gripped us, and we slap our loved one's cheek. The karmic result will be pain and hatred.

This is a very simple example of the law of karma, which is not unlike a law of physics. Throwing a pebble in a pond will not produce fire. Nonvirtuous actions will not produce lasting happiness. The bodhisattva warrior cultivates virtue from a very intelligent perspective. I and others want to be happy. Virtue produces happiness; nonvirtue produces unhappiness. Looking at it that way, what would you choose?

Generally speaking, a virtuous activity makes us lighter, both in the sense of feeling more lightweight and in the sense of having a quality of illumination. A nonvirtuous activity, although it may bring some immediate pleasure, will make us feel heavy, dark, and somewhat hidden in the long run. Our inherent wisdom might well poke through while we are engaged in a nonvirtuous activity with the thought "I wonder how long I can get away with this."

We do have inherent wisdom in us. It has never been polluted by our confusion. It is the source of inexhaustible richness. A traditional example is of a person living in abject poverty who doesn't realize that right underneath them in the ground is a vein of pure gold. If they're fortunate, someone with insight and kindness passes by and says, "There is a vein of pure gold right below the surface here, and this is how you dig." The poor person follows the instructions and uncovers the richness that has been there all along.

Although we have innate goodness and wisdom within us, it is of no use to ourselves or others if we can't recognize it and access it. It is like the gold hidden in the ground. The journey of realization, the digging, begins with gentleness. Gentleness brings openness. Mindfulness and awareness inform openness, and the clarity and warmth of openness uncover wisdom.

Because it is your own wisdom and not somebody else's, having loyalty to wisdom is trustworthy. It is beneficial because it illuminates what to cultivate and what to refrain from to bring happiness and peace to yourself, those around you, and the world.

When we experience the truth and goodness of the path, we naturally feel grateful to those who had the insight and kindness to let us know about the gold and how to reach it. An unbroken lineage of warrior bodhisattvas has passed the living experience of bodhichitta from generation to generation for twenty-five hundred years. We appreciate the love and loyalty of these men and women.

We each have that same wisdom within us, like a sun in our hearts. We possess a radiating confidence and peacefulness that illuminates what we should say and do in order to find happiness. Uncovering, assessing, and cultivating confidence in our own wisdom is the purpose of all of the skillful means we have discussed in this book. These tools are for learning to open and trust yourself. The purpose of all of the teachings of the Buddha is to awaken your inherent wisdom so that it can shine and illuminate the darkness of ignorance.

BEING TRUE

Another way to express the meaning of loyalty is *being true*. We could talk about being true to our partner or about being true to gentleness, openness, and wisdom. Or we could just talk about being true, without any "to."

Being true is an interesting turn of phrase, because if we reverse it, we get *true being*. True being is perhaps as close as we can come to a description of the fruit of the path of the warrior bodhisattva. Through the skillful means and wisdom of the path, the warrior has learned to be true in speech and action. "The key to warriorship," says Chögyam Trungpa, "is not being afraid of who you are."

Because you already are who you are, because you

are already being, you don't have to become something to be true. As Avalokitesvara, the bodhisattva of compassion, teaches, "There is no attainment and no nonattainment." In other words, we don't have to get anything or not get anything; we already are basic goodness. Although we need to apply the skillful means of the path, the realization of basic goodness is ultimately the result of relaxing and opening in the present moment, because it is already here. Taking this attitude from the beginning is helpful in not being too hard on ourselves.

The journey of warriorship begins with friendship with ourself. The Four Limitless Ones give us the opportunity to open our hearts and our minds. The six far-gone actions provide the skillful means and the wisdom to engage openness in our everyday lives. The path of the far-gone actions is the progressive cultivation of bravery and uncovering confidence in openness and confidence in ourselves, the confidence to open into and let go into the windhorse of basic goodness. A person with windhorse has confidence and can ride the ups and downs and coincidences of life. When we have the confidence of windhorse, we can accomplish our purposes. Because we are connected to the world around us, we attract auspiciousness—the right situation at the right time.

When we perceive ourselves as the center of the universe from the point of view of ego, we experience duality—I and everything else are two separate things. If we perceive ourselves as the center of the universe from the point of view of egolessness, we experience mandala. *Mandala* means that there is a center and a fringe or perimeter. Experientially, this means being present (the center) and aware of the universe around us (the fringe). In a mandala, these are not two separate things; rather, there is a sense of the whole and great equanimity.

Because ego perpetuates the illusion of separation, the experience of mandala is hidden from ego's perspective. From ego's point of view, the center is always most important, so the fringe—the field of our awareness, the world we live in, and the people we share it with—can be ignored or used only for our own benefit. Ego by nature has a limited and short-term perspective.

Ego and *egolessness* are not ultimate terms—there is not a line somewhere that clearly divides the two states of being. In reality, there are many combinations and gradations. When decisions are made for short-term gratification without regard to potential long-term harm, the perspective is more that of ego. When decisions are based on long-range benefit that will continue for generations to come, well, there is more egolessness there.

In the world today, we are seeing more and more often the harmful effects, often long lasting, of decisions based on short-term gain. However, the awareness of this is our salvation, because once we realize it, we can change it. We can have greater vision. There can still be ego involved, but it could become less and less over time. That is why it's important to not be afraid of who we are. Although our true nature is egoless, we all have ego. Whether we are walking on the path of ego or the path of egolessness depends on where we place our allegiance, our loyalty.

In the Shambhala teachings, there is a term that is used to refer to and describe true being: *authentic presence*. *Authentic* means genuine; *presence* is the state or fact of existing. Thus *authentic presence* means genuine, true existence. We are not talking about the true existence of ego, but the true existence of what lies right beneath ego's games: the sun of basic goodness.

The Tibetan word for "authentic presence" is wangtang, which literally means "field of power." Because there is no separation or "optical delusion," because there is the openness of bodhichitta, the power of a person with authentic presence is connected with the power of things as they are. Or perhaps we can say that truth is fully manifesting on the spot. There is not another truth somewhere else.

You can feel this when you interact with a person who has authentic presence. As Chögyam Trungpa described the experience, "There is some sense of 'real trueness' taking place." Because something true and honest and real is happening, it feels good. Even if you are only talking about the weather, it seems good and worthwhile.

Such is the fruit, or result, of the skillful means and the wisdom of the bodhisattva path. When we take a journey, we usually focus on arriving at our destination, our goal. But in the journey of a bodhisattva, the goal is reached all along the way, as the journey unfolds. Effortlessly, authentic presence dawns in the warrior bodhisattvas who exert themselves on the path.

This is beneficial for everyone: those closest to you and all beings who call this earth home. Being true, we can bring our world back into harmony. That is the great spiritual challenge of our time. It is possible, and it is up to each of us.

It is my aspiration that something in this little book will be helpful in your life. Living our lives with love and loyalty, the circle of love and wisdom that was set in motion by the Buddha and other great beings can continue to expand on this earth, and bring peace, prosperity, and equanimity to all who live here.

It is to this great vision that this little book is dedicated.

Acknowledgments

I would like to thank Jennifer Holder for the beautiful blank writing book and her gentle encouragement to take the next step once I filled it in. Who knows if anything would have happened if it hadn't been for her generosity?

At Shambhala Publications, I would like to thank Emily Bower for seeing the potential in my first draft, for her friendship, and for pointing me in the right direction. I would also like to thank Peter Turner very much for his astute feedback and guidance.

I was very fortunate to work with Eden Steinberg as the editor of this book. She was a taskmaster and made me dig deep. When I needed encouragement, she had the right words to keep me going, Her suggestions showed a deep understanding of the Buddha's teaching. Her editing skills made me enjoy reading my own writing. Her influence is on every page of this book, and I would like to share the credit.

Notes

BOOK EPIGRAPH

It is in this way that we must train ourselves

From the *Samyutta-nikaya sutta,* as excerpted in *The Buddha Speaks: A Book of Guidance from the Buddhist Scriptures,* edited by Anne Bancroft (Boston: Shambhala Publications, 2010).

CHAPTER 1: BEING YOUR OWN BEST FRIEND

basic goodness

Chögyam Trungpa, *Shambhala: The Sacred Path of the Warrior* (Boston: Shambhala Publications, 1984), 35–41.

the natural, clear, and uncluttered state of our being

Sakyong Mipham, *Ruling Your World: Ancient Strategies for Modern Life* (New York: Morgan Road Books, 2005), 1.

CHAPTER 2: LOVING YOUR PARTNER

"Being in love does not mean possessing the other person"

Chögyam Trungpa, *1981 Seminary Transcripts: Hinayana-Mahayana* (Boulder, Colo.: Vajradhatu Publications, 1981), 67.

a journey outward. It's very quick, like the lightbulb flash

Chögyam Trungpa, *Glimpses of Mahayana* (Halifax, Nova Scotia, Canada: Vajradhatu Publications, 2001), 29–40.

CHAPTER 3: LOVING YOUR CHILD

"Do not seek perfection in a changing world. Instead perfect your love"

Master Sengstan, as quoted in Jack Kornfield, *Buddha's Little Instruction Book* (New York: Bantam Books, 1994).

"Every child needs periodic genuine encounters"

Dorothy Corkille Briggs, *Your Child's Self-Esteem* (New York: Broadway Books, 1970), 64.

CHAPTER 4: THE POWER OF A WISH

"a flash of lightning on a dark night"

Shantideva, *Bodhisattvacharyavatara* (Sanskrit), "A Guide to the Way of a Bodhisattva," chapter 1, verse 5, in Pema Chödrön, *No Time to Lose: A Timely Guide to the Way of the Bodhisattva* (Boston: Shambhala Publications, 2005), 5.

everybody is equal because we are all unique

Shunryu Suzuki, *Branching Streams Flow in the Darkness: Zen Talks on the Sandokai* (Los Angeles: University of California Press, 1999), 41–42.

Dissolve the boundaries

Pema Chödrön, *The Places That Scare You: A Guide to Fearlessness in Difficult Times* (Boston: Shambhala Publications, 2002), 46.

CHAPTER 5: TRUE BRAVERY

opening to and welcoming others as they are

Chögyam Trungpa, *Mudra* (Berkeley, Calif.: Shambhala Publications, 1972), 102.

panoramic awareness

Chögyam Trungpa, *Cutting through Spiritual Materialism* (Boston: Shambhala Publications, 1987), 167–68.

"the means of stabilizing oneself within the framework of seeing relationships"

Trungpa, *Mudra,* 103.

CHAPTER 6: LOVE AND LOYALTY

"We can have loyalty to our own gentleness"

Chögyam Trungpa, *Collected Kalapa Assemblies* (Halifax, Nova Scotia, Canada: Vajradhatu Publications, 2006) 402.

"the ability to ride the inherent strength and vitality of our awareness"

Mipham, *Ruling Your World,* 32.

"Wisdom and compassion begin with cultivating discernment"
Ibid., 48.

"There is a vein of pure gold right below the surface"
> Arya Maitreya, *Buddha Nature* (Ithaca, N.Y.: Snow Lion Publications, 2000), 155–56.

"The key to warriorship"
> Trungpa, *Shambhala*, 28.

"There is no attainment and no nonattainment"
> Avalokitesvara, *The Sutra of the Heart of Transcendent Knowledge* (Halifax, Nova Scotia: Nalanda Translation Committee).

"There is some sense of 'real trueness' taking place"
> Trungpa, *Collected Kalapa Assemblies*, 41.

Resources

BOOKS

The Sutra of the Heart of Transcendent Knowledge. Halifax, Nova Scotia: Nalanda Translation Committee.

Bancroft, Anne, ed. *The Buddha Speaks: A Book of Guidance from the Buddhist Scriptures.* Boston: Shambhala Publications, 2010.

Briggs, Dorothy Corkille. *Your Child's Self-Esteem.* New York: Broadway Books, 1970.

Chödrön, Pema. *No Time to Lose: A Timely Guide to the Way of the Bodhisattva* Boston: Shambhala Publications, 2005.

————. *The Places That Scare You: A Guide to Fearlessness in Difficult Times.* Boston: Shambhala Publications, 2002.

————. *Taking the Leap: Freeing Ourselves from Old Habits and Fears.* Boston: Shambhala Publications, 2009.

Kornfield, Jack. *Buddha's Little Instruction Book.* New York: Bantam Books, 1994.

Maitreya, Arya. *Buddha Nature.* Ithaca, N.Y.: Snow Lion Publications, 2000.

Mipham, Sakyong. *Ruling Your World: Ancient Strategies for Modern Life.* New York: Morgan Road Books, 2005.

————. *Turning the Mind into an Ally.* New York: Riverhead Books, 2003.

Suzuki, Shunryu. *Branching Streams Flow in the Darkness: Zen Talks on the Sandokai.* Los Angeles: University of California Press, 1999.

Trungpa, Chögyam. *Collected Kalapa Assemblies.* Halifax, Nova Scotia, Canada: Vajradhatu Publications, 2006.

————. *Cutting through Spiritual Materialism.* Boston: Shambhala Publications, 1987.

————. *Glimpses of Mahayana.* Halifax, Nova Scotia, Canada: Vajradhatu Publications, 2001.

————. *Mudra.* Berkeley, Calif., and London: Shambhala Publications, 1972.

————. *1981 Seminary Transcripts: Hinayana-Mahayana.* Boulder, Colo.: Vajradhatu Publications, 1981.

————. *Shambhala: The Sacred Path of the Warrior.* Boston: Shambhala Publications, 1984.

OTHER RESOURCES

For information regarding meditation instruction or inquiries about a practice center near you, please contact one of the following:

Shambhala International
1084 Tower Road
Halifax, Nova Scotia
Canada B3H 2Y5
www.shambhala.org (This website contains video, audio, and printed teachings by Chögyam Trungpa, Sakyong

Mipham, and Pema Chödrön, as well as information about more than two hundred centers affiliated with Shambhala.)

Shambhala Europe
Kartäuserwall 20
50678 Cologne
Germany
www.shambhala-europe.org

Karmê Chöling (retreat center)
369 Patneaude Lane
Barnet, Vermont 05821
www.karmecholing.org

Shambhala Mountain Center
151 Shambhala Way
Red Feather Lakes, Colorado 80545
www.shambhalamountain.org

Dechen Chöling (retreat center)
Mas Marvent
87700 St. Yrieix sous Aixe
France
www.dechencholing.org

Dorje Denma Ling (retreat center)
2280 Balmoral Road
Tatamagouche, Nova Scotia
Canada B0K 1V0
www.dorjedenmaling.org

Gampo Abbey
Pleasant Bay, Nova Scotia
Canada B0E 2P0
www.gampoabbey.org

Meditation cushions and other supplies are available through:

Samadhi Cushions
30 Church Street
Barnet, Vermont 05821
phone: (800) 331-7751
www.samadhistore.com

The only accredited Buddhist-inspired university in North America:

Naropa University
2130 Arapahoe Avenue
Boulder, Colorado 80302
phone: (303) 444-0202
www.naropa.edu

Books, audio recordings, and video recordings of talks and seminars by Chögyam Trungpa and Pema Chödrön are available from:

Shambhala Media
3008 Oxford Street, Suite 201
Halifax, Nova Scotia
Canada B3L 2W5
phone (toll free): 888-450-1002
www.shambhalamedia.org

The *Shambhala Sun* is a bimonthly Buddhist magazine founded by Chögyam Trungpa Rinpoche. The magazine also contains a listing of centers that offer meditation programs and instruction in many Buddhist traditions, throughout North America. For a subscription or sample copy, go to www.shambhalasun.com.

Shambhala Sun
P.O. Box 469095
Escondido, California 92046-9095
phone: (877) 786-1950
www.shambhalasun.com

Buddhadharma: The Practitioner's Quarterly is published four times each year. A listing of meditation centers offering instruction can be found in the journal. For a subscription or sample copy, go to www.thebuddhadharma.com.

Buddhadharma
P.O. Box 3377
Champlain, New York 12919-9871
www.thebuddhadharma.com

About the Author

MOH HARDIN is a senior teacher (*acharya*) in the Shambhala Buddhist lineage. He lives with his wife, Cynde Grieve, in Halifax, Nova Scotia. Together they teach and work with the Shambhala Centers in Canada's Atlantic provinces—Nova Scotia, New Brunswick, Prince Edward Island, and Newfoundland—and in the United States in Texas and Louisiana. For more information, visit www.shambhala.org/teachers/acharya/mhardin.